Patrice -
  Thank you for always being there
for me. I love how our friendship
has evolved!
          I love you xo
          [signature]

# Bali Girl

# Bali Girl

*A leap of faith into spiritual awakening*

Based on a true story

By

Anne Latour

Printed in the United States of America

Library of Congress Cataloging-in-Publication Data is on file at the Library of Congress, Washington DC.

ISBN 978-1-304-99556-8

Published by Anne Latour
www.annelatour.com

Unless otherwise indicated, Scripture quotations are from the Holy Bible, New International Version®. NIV®

Events, locales and conversations are based on author's memories. In order to maintain the anonymity in some instances, names have been changed. Some details as in physical properties, occupations and places may have been changed.

Cover Design by Jessica Suderno www.DelightMeDesign.com
Photos taken by Alex Lunoe. All rights reserved.
Prayer by Joy Teragli. All rights reserved.
Editing by Christine L. Niles
http://www.book-editing.com/book-consultant-bios/christine-le/index.html

Ordering information: Special discounts are available on quantity purchases by non-profit organizations, corporations, associations, educators, and others. For details, contact the publisher.
U.S. Trade bookstores and wholesalers: Please fax request to: (888) 712-8406 or email to: info@privasicuro.com

# BLESSINGS

First and foremost I thank my best friend and savior, God.

My journey has been long, with many people to thank, but most importantly I would like to express my love and gratitude to my mother, Carol. Dad loved you with all his heart, he is proud of the mother you are, and he watches over you every day with love. To my brother Scott, an amazing man coming into his own. We never know what type of ball God will throw us, but somehow you always know how to catch it. I am proud that you are my brother. To my sister Joy: you are the best friend I will ever have, the big sister you will always be, and the inspiration that never stops. God has a bigger plan for you—trust Him always. And to my twin sister Beth, my other half: we were born as one but with two separate paths. I admire your fight to be independent from the world. To my dearest son Grant: you are a gift that keeps on giving. As much as I would love to believe that you belong to me, you are all God's. I am honored that God has given me the opportunity to be your mother, your model of faith and hope. I promise to do my best. You will do big things and make God very proud. Always be you and honor only God first.

I learned a lot about friends during my first weeks of recovery. My special acknowledgements go out to the friends who showed up even when I did not call on them. Renee, you are an inspiration to me, both spiritually and professionally. Thank you for always being my sunshine. Patrice, we have the same God no matter how we look at it. Thank you for always being real. To my friend Jeff: thank you for keeping me present. Your continued positive outlook on life inspires me. Stephanie, sometimes it takes hard times to see who true friends are, and I love you for that. To Vanessa: if it weren't for you, everyone would be in the dark. Thank you for always being here for me. For my friend Tatiana: Some time we have to lose in order to gain. Thanks for cheering me on. And for Dave, you will always have a place in my heart. Thank you for teaching me so much, I truly appreciate you.

To my friends who live so far away but offered to be there for me: Traci, you will always be my son's aunt, no matter the circumstances. I cherish our friendship and look forward to our growth through Christ. To Richelle: we are soul sisters. Thank you for the continued prayer, support, and inspiration through it all. To my heroes, Alex and Michael: I cannot thank you enough. Although we have miles separating us, I feel closer to you now more than ever before. Thank you for stepping up and being the best friends a person could ever have.

I thank God for my copy editor, Christine Niles. You are an incredible woman and an inspiring person. Thank you for putting up with my crazy nuances and helping guide me through this process. To Jessica: Thank you for all of your professional opinions and support. I look forward to watching you grow in faith with God.

To all of those who brought meals and helped out in specials ways, thank you from the bottom of my heart.

As I have found along my journey, God brings people into our lives for a reason. Sometimes we will never know what those reasons are, but if you are fortunate enough to find out, be sure to let your special someone know how much you appreciate them . . .

# ~ contents ~

# the drugging

I just a finished a meeting and am heading down pacific coast highway towards Huntington Beach to pick up my nine-year-old son Cruz up from school. It's a beautiful spring day, palm trees swaying in the breeze and flowers in full bloom. I look out the driver's side window of my Mercedes to see the ocean. Every time I see it, it makes me realize how blessed I am. I had never imagined that I would be living here in Southern California. I came from a small town in Central Oregon with a population of ten thousand, most of whom came from generations and generations of people who lived there before them. My dad had moved our family there after buying a small trucking company. Even before moving we lived in the suburbs, just outside of Portland. Growing up in Oregon gave me a chance to learn a lot about myself and the value of nature. Although I loved living near my family, I had always wanted to spread my wings and experience new places. Just after school I took a huge leap of faith and moved to Southern California to take a job with a CPA firm. Living in Southern California has given me a chance to meet new people and develop my career in accounting.

Several years after planting my roots here, I got married to a man much older than me. It took me nine years to realize that we were two completely different people. I had been too young when I married him, not knowing who I was and, of course, not knowing who I'd want to spend the rest of my life with. Although the marriage didn't work out, I received the best gift possible: my son Cruz. It took several years of hell during the divorce process, but thankfully my ex-husband and I are now amicable when it comes to raising our son Cruz.

Shortly after the divorce, I rented a really cool multi-level condo near the beach. The condo complex has a pool, which tends to be the gathering place for our neighborhood. I've made some phenomenal friendships with some of my neighbors, which makes for a nice time during the holidays.

Trips back home to Oregon are tough while sharing custody of Cruz, so we usually end up at our neighbor's house.

One of my passions is running on the bike path adjacent to the beach, but on the days that I have Cruz, we like taking our dog down to the dog beach. Huntington Beach is one of the few places in Southern California that allows dogs on the beach, and our dog London loves playing in the sand.

As I get closer to the school, I get frustrated thinking back to earlier in the day when my ex-husband called to tell me that he needed me to pick Cruz up from school. It literally took the wind out of my sails. It was good news and bad news. Good news, because I would have Cruz for the weekend; bad news, because I would have to cancel my evening tomorrow with my friend Dave.

Dave and I have been dating on and off for several years now, but he hasn't been able to commit to an exclusive relationship. Showing up every few of weeks seems to work for him, but it leaves me feeling empty. He's incredibly attractive, standing tall at 6' 6', with broad shoulders and dark skin. His greenish brown eyes look right through me. Every time I see him, my heart flips. I haven't brought him around Cruz much yet because our relationship has been so inconsistent. Dave doesn't know if he could ever settle down with anyone. He's a free spirit, traveling all the time with his business and committed to helping his sickly parents who live in the Portland area. It's annoying because I really like him, but I want to be with a man who wants to be in a fully committed relationship.

I make the turn down Main Street and smile. I can't help but be happy seeing everyone walk around in sundresses and flip flops, standing around ice cream shops and stores. Although Huntington Beach has a population of two hundred thousand, it seems much smaller when I am downtown. The boutique clothing stores, surf shops, and beach bars are fun places for the locals to gather. Cruz and I like people watching on Sundays, after church.

As I pull up to Seacliff Elementary I see Cruz standing near a giant palm tree talking with some of his buddies. The school is fairly new, built only fourteen years ago. It has a unique architecture to it with a ranch-style,

# the drugging

stucco look. There are five grade levels, with small class sizes, giving it private school feel. We've been blessed the four years we've been here.

Cruz spots me from the sidewalk and runs up to the car. "Mom, I got an A on my math test!" he yells as he opens the passenger side door. "Do I get a new video game, Mom, do I?"

Cruz is a brilliant kid with nothing else on his mind but video games. I don't mind, because he gets good grades and I see it as a way for him to unwind from the pressures of school.

"Ok, but you need to make it quick," I say, giving him a half-hug over the center console. "I have work I need to finish up before five o'clock."

We drive to his favorite game store and pick up the latest in his favorite battle series.

As we pull up our street, I spot Toby and Bridget backing out of their garage. I wave and smile; it reminds me that we will be seeing them at the BBQ and swim party later tonight, after Cruz's football game. Toby and his wife Bridget live a couple condos down from ours. Their daughter Sabrina is nine years old, the same age as Cruz. We spend a lot of time with them on the weekends, riding our bikes or just hanging out. They introduced us to the church we attend; Bridget came from a similar Christian background as I did, so it makes for a good friendship.

After getting home, Cruz goes to play his new video game, and I go straight to my office. I started an accounting business just after my divorce, so my work allows me to do a lot from my home. I am blessed, because my home office has a view of the ocean and Pacific Coast Highway, sometimes making it hard to concentrate. Our condo has a homey, beach feel to it. My older sister Olivia had flown down from Oregon to help me decorate it after my divorce. Being that everything was going to be new to Cruz in the midst of a life-changing event, I wanted things to be cozy and inviting to him. I hadn't been able to decide on which couch to buy, so I ended up with two. I've been able to make the best out of it and create two separate family rooms, one overlooking the ocean and one in the back of the house where the kitchen is.

As soon as I wrap my work up, I head downstairs to get Cruz ready for his football game. It's the last game of the season. "Hey bud, we need to leave. We gotta' be out the door in thirty minutes."

As I walk into the TV room, he's laid back on the couch playing his video game wearing only his football jersey, underwear, jock strap, and one blue sock. "Dude, really?" I say opening the refrigerator. "Finish getting dressed—and then play until it's time to leave."

Cruz rolls his eyes and sets down his controller. "Ok, Mom."

I grab some bottles of water and throw them in a back pack. His football games are fairly quick, lasting only one hour, but it gets hot at times, so hydration is important. After Cruz finishes getting dressed, we head out to the football field.

We get lucky and pull into a parking spot just in front of the high school. I jump out and grab my folding lawn chair; the field they're playing on today doesn't have benches. As we walk up to the field, I can see the moms standing together chatting, dressed a little more nicely than usual, which is normal on the last game of the season. This is when all the pictures are taken that will end up on their walls for years to come. I had decided to wear my tailored white cargo pants, turquoise blouse, and brown leather flip flops. The wind is slightly blowing and now I'm wishing I had put my hair up.

As we walk up to the field, Cruz starts running across, yelling, "Pool party at my house!"

One of the moms turns to me as I get closer. "Are you sure you know what you're doing letting all these boys swim at your pool?" The other ladies laugh.

"Yes, it's okay," I respond laughing. "I love having parties—and besides, the pool isn't at my house; it's a community pool."

One of the other moms joins in the conversation. "I'm all set, and I have the sodas in the car," she says. "Are you sure you don't need anything else?"

I sit down in my lawn chair. "Yep, we're all good. The pizzas will arrive twenty minutes after we get to the pool, and I've already mixed the margaritas." I look down the field and see a man standing on the sideline I haven't seen before. I'm not much for judging, but something doesn't look right about him. He is tall, about 6'5", with tattoos down the sides of his arms and up around his neck. He's wearing some nice clothes, but something isn't right about him. I sit there pondering . . .

I guess I'm looking a little too long, because he turns and looks straight at me and then looks away. *Darn it!* That's not good. He probably thinks I'm checking him out. I look away, but he has started walking towards me. I turn to start a conversation with the moms, but they're already deep in one . . . *Shoot. What do I do?* I can sense him getting closer to me. I glance quickly up and realize that—yes—he's coming straight toward me.

"Hi," he says. "Is your son playing tonight?"

I immediately stand up and put out my hand. "Hi, yes . . . umm, he's about to play right now," I say, shaking his hand. "I'm Anne. Is your son playing, too?" His presence is creepy. There's something odd about him.

He turns to the field. "Nice to meet you, Anne. I'm Eddie—and no, I'm just here visiting my friend Terrance."

Now it makes sense to me; Cruz's coach is Terrance. This guy is here for Coach Terrance; perhaps he's not a weirdo. I sit down and look up at him. "Terrance is my son's coach. Where are you visiting from?"

He looks down at me, his head blocking the sun. "I live in the Bay area, and I'm just down for the night."

"Really? Just one night?" I think to myself how odd that seems. "That's a fast trip."

"Yes, just for the night." He stands there a little while longer, and eventually walks back up the field.

The game ends with a high scoring tie, but the kids don't seem to mind—they're all excited for the after-party at the pool. Cruz and I rush back to the house in order to set up. We pull into the garage and get out of the car.

"Cruz—run upstairs and change into your swim suit," I say, opening the door into the house. "I'll meet you back down here. I need you to help me carry some things to the pool." I run upstairs and mix together two pitchers of margaritas, making sure not to make it too strong—it's a kid's pool party, after all. I don't want things getting out of hand.

My phone vibrates on the counter; I look over to see it's a text from my friend Rhonda. It reads: *Going to dinner with Rick; we'll stop by your pool party later.* I've known Rhonda for ten years now; we are like two peas in a pod. We do just about everything together. I met her just after Cruz was born, and shortly after that she became my friend. I consider her family, almost like she's my sister. She's ten years younger than me, but we get along so well. Rhonda just started dating Rick a few weeks ago after meeting him on an online dating website. We've been on a couple group dates together; he seems like a great guy, almost too good for Rhonda. She's a great girl, but I think she has some growing up to do before settling down with a man.

I wipe my hands with a towel on the counter and quickly text her back. *Have fun and don't drink too much! I want you to bring the* Patrón *from my house when you get here. We'll have a couple shots once the party starts winding down.* Patrón is like water for me; I can drink a lot of it and not get drunk or sick. For some reason my body metabolizes it much more quickly than any other alcohol. It's my go-to drink when I'm watching my calories or when I'm out at bars. It's easier and safer to take a quick shot than to walk around with a drink in my hand that could get poisoned.

I stuff the pitchers of margaritas into the cooler and shove some limes down the side, yelling to Cruz as I run downstairs to the garage, "Hurry up! We need to open the pool door for everyone!"

He comes running up behind me. "What do you want me to carry, Mom?" He opens the door for me.

"Thanks, bud! Can you open the pool door with the key?" I point to the key sitting on the tool bench.

He grabs it and runs out of the garage toward the pool. I step outside of the garage and press the code into the key pad on the side of the house to close the garage door.

I walk as fast as I can to the pool. Everybody is probably already there, but I want to have everything set up for them. As I walk into the pool area, I see that Cruz has propped open the door. Down by the hot tub are a couple of parents setting down their bags. I walk past some neighbors, nod hello, and arrive at our two round tables.

"Is anyone up for a margarita?" I ask, as I set the cooler down and lift up the drinks. Several of the parents come rushing over and start pouring. I pour myself one and set it down on the table, looking around the edge of the pool through the lattice fence to see if the pizza guy is here. Just as I turn around, I see him out of the corner of my eye. I pay him, grab the boxes, and bring them back to the tables as a trail of wet boys follows behind me.

"Give me a second, guys." After I've arranged the pizzas around the table, I lift the tops. "Here you go—have at it!" The boys start tearing into the food. They eat it like it's the only thing they've eaten in days. I look up at the entrance to the pool and see the coach walking in with his friend Eddie. There's just something about him that I don't like. I think to myself that I should probably watch him around the kids.

Coach Terrance walks up with a cooler of beer and sets it down next to the tables on the grass, his wife not too far behind lugging a big cloth bag and some cleats. Both Terrance and Eddie open their beers and start talking to the assistant coach, Ken. Ken has really been the coach for most of the season, making it to all the practices and games. Coach Terrance seemed to flake out on a lot of team work. Ken is a hardworking family man, married to an adorable wife, and he seems to be a great dad to his three kids. During the season I could see a struggle of communication with both coaches; I felt for Coach Ken because he did all the work but got no credit.

I look down for my cup and can't find it, so I pour myself another drink. As I'm sipping it, I walk around the pool making sure the kids aren't harassing my neighbors. All is good. The boys are floating around on a raft that someone must have brought. I walk back to the table and sit down with the moms.

"It's so nice for the season to be over," I say, setting my cup down in front of me. All the women say "yes" in unison, and we all toast. I sit there for a while watching the kids, overhearing the moms talk about next season. I don't want to join the conversation because I'm not sure if Cruz wants to play again; he had expressed interest in doing baseball, so I thought we should discuss it before committing to another season of flag football.

The sun is starting to go down and it's getting chilly. Thank God I had wrapped my black running jacket around my waist before leaving the house. I put it on and look up to see my friend Rhonda walking up with my bottle of *Patrón* and her new man, Rick. She sets it on the table and I give her a hug. "Nice to finally see you," I say.

I look up at Rick with a smile. "Hey, there." Rhonda picks up a cup and immediately starts to pour a shot of tequila into the cup.

"I need this!" I laugh and grab a cup, and not to be rude to everyone else standing there, I offer, "Anyone want a shot?" Two moms raise their hand, along with Coach Terrance and his friend Eddie. I look over at Ken; it looks as if he didn't hear me. "Hey, Ken! Do you want a shot of *Patrón*?"

He happily responds, "*Patrón*? Heck yeah!" I start to pour everyone about an ounce each. I hand them out and lift my own. "To a great season — thanks, coaches!" We all toast.

I sit down with Rhonda and chat a bit about her date while eating pizza. I can see Rick and Ken talking over at the tables and laughing about something. I look around to see that the kids are doing well, not making too much of a ruckus. I don't see Coach Terrance and his friend, though; maybe they stepped out to smoke. I had seen Eddie smoking earlier at the field.

Just as I get up to go to the bathroom, Coach Terrance and Eddie show up to the table asking for another shot. I ask the moms if they want another one and they say no. Rick and Ken, however, are game, so I start to pour another round. Just as I'm about to grab the last one for myself, Eddie picks up a drink from the table and offers it to me. "Here — you can have this one. Terrance chickened out on the last round." I look at Coach Terrance and he chuckles as Eddie holds it out across the table. My stomach turns and I look at Rhonda; she shrugs her shoulders.

"Ok. I guess so." I grab the drink and look into the cup; it looks like a lot. I quickly pour a little bit out into Rhonda's cup.

"Hey," she protests, "I already have enough!" We all laugh and toast again.

I sit down and Rhonda follows in the chair next to mine. The guys are still talking at the table and the kids are in the pool. I am beginning to feel very relaxed . . . Suddenly, Cruz is standing in front of me. "Mom, Mom! Are you drunk?"

I laugh. "Of course not, bud—I'm not drunk."

He gives me a wet hug. "Okaaaaaay—it's just that you look drunk," and he runs off. I get up from my chair and stumble as I see Cruz running out of the pool area. I try to run after him but I keep falling; things seem blurry and yet far away. *Ouch!* I hit the tree outside of the pool, my face hurts . . . I stumble into the street. My upper body seems to be moving faster than my legs.

**********

*Ding Ding Ding!* My cell phone rings. I sit straight up in bed. I look at the clock. What the hell—it's eight a.m.! I grab my phone and it's a text from Cruz: *Mom.* My heart is racing; I'm feeling faint.

I immediately call him. "Cruz, where are you?" I get up out of bed; my legs feel like jello. I hit the wall. *Damn—that hurt.* I hit the other wall. I can't seem to walk straight or keep myself upright. I don't feel sick or hung over. This isn't making any sense.

"Mom, you were drunk," he says in a little whisper.

"Oh my gosh, Cruz; I am so sorry," is all I could say as I'm stumbling throughout the house. "What happened?" I look in every room; nobody is here and the sun is shining through the windows.

"Mom, you were so drunk. Neighbor John came over and tried to help you. Mom, you ran into his front gate after you hit a tree. You walked into the dryer. I was afraid you broke your nose!" He pauses. "Mom, you tried to pet London and fell over the gate." London is our two-year-old Rottweiler.

All I can say is I'm sorry over and over again into the phone. I have a big lump in my throat and I'm feeling scared. "Where are you?"

"Mom, I had to call Dad. You scared me; you almost fell backwards on the steps . . . and Mom, you threw up!" He says, a little more loudly now.

"I did?" Tears start flowing down my cheeks. How could I do this? How did I get so drunk that I did this to him? *Oh, God, how do I ever make it up to him?*

"Mom, you threw up on Coach Ken; he was helping you in the bathroom. Mom, his wife was so mad."

I slowly make my way back up to the bedroom and sit on my bed. "I am so sorry."

Cruz breathes into the phone. "Mom, don't ever do that again!"

I look around my bedroom; everything seems to be in place. "I promise, Cruz, never again . . . Where was Rhonda?"

"She was drunk, too, Mom; her boyfriend had to take her home. Mom, your eyes were weird; you looked like a monster."

"Cruz, let me talk to your dad." I can hear him handing the phone over to Jeff.

"Hello," his deep voice comes over the phone.

"What the heck happened last night?" I ask him.

"You were drunk. Your neighbor John called me because Cruz was too afraid to stay with you last night."

Now I'm really sick to my stomach. "What? John called you?" My neighbor John is a nice guy; he lives with his wife who is an ER doctor. They frequent our neighborhood barbeques often.

"Yes—and I don't like getting called by a strange man that tells me my son is in his house."

My heart sinks. "Jeff, I am so sorry. I don't remember anything."

"It's okay; I told Cruz you were drunk and that you would never do it again."

"Jeff, this is scary. I seriously don't know what happened."

Then it hits me: I must have been drugged! That would make sense. I've never passed out like that waking up to what I'm feeling right now.

"Don't worry about it. Rest up. I'll keep Cruz for the weekend."

I hang up the phone and quickly text Cruz: *I love you.*

He responds, *I love you so much, Mom.*

I lie back onto the pillows against the headboard. My head hurts. I quickly text Rhonda. *What happened last night?* I stare at the ceiling, dozing off.

*Ding!* My phone rings. I sit up and look down as it falls in my lap. I must have fallen asleep with it. Just as I swipe the phone to unlock it, everything hits me. I look at the time; it's four o'clock and my bedroom doesn't look bright anymore. I'm so mad at myself. How did that happen last night? My stomach and throat begin to knot up again. I look at my phone and see that it's a text from Rhonda. *Call me.* I get out of bed and try to walk to the bathroom. I'm feeling a little more mobile now and only bump into one wall. As I walk into the bathroom, I notice that there's vomit on the bathroom wall, next to the toilet. Cruz was right—I did throw up. I just don't remember it. Odd. I use the toilet and then go back to bed, dialing Rhonda's number.

"Hello?"

"Oh my God, Rhonda—Cruz called me this morning . . ." I pause to take a gulp of water from the glass next to my bed. "I think I was drugged. Cruz said I was falling all over the place and threw up . . . Rhonda! I don't remember anything. The last thing I remember is taking a shot at the pool."

"Anne, you kept falling down and I remember Cruz crying and yelling at you; he was mad that you were drunk. I tried to comfort him, but I couldn't."

"What else do you remember? I don't remember anything."

"I don't remember a lot—I guess I drank too much, too."

"But I thought you said you didn't drink anything at dinner—all you had were the two shots of *Patrón.*"

She replies with a low voice, "I know; I was thinking that was strange."

"Rhonda, I think we were drugged."

"What?"

"Yeah." I take another gulp of water. My head still hurts and I'm really thirsty.

"Anne, I slept with Rick last night," she whispers. Rhonda had recently vowed along with me not to sleep with a guy we're dating until after at least three months. I know that she was convicted just as much as I was to stick to it, so it seemed odd that she would have sex with Rick on her third date.

"Seriously?" I ask.

"Yessssss, and Anne, I don't remember it." I could sense that she seemed scared.

"Rhonda, we were drugged." I try to recreate the night in my head and I just can't think. Then it hits me. The coach's friend, Eddie—he had given me a shot from the table and I had shared it with Rhonda. That has to be it! I didn't drink anything that would have been left alone to be tainted. But why would he do that?

"The only thing we shared last night was that shot."

"What?"

"Yeah, do you remember when Eddie, that tall weird guy, handed me a shot on the last round?"

"Oh, yeah—I do." Her voice gets louder. "You poured some of it into my cup."

"Yeah, I'm sorry." All of a sudden I feel bad that she was drugged, too. I know she really wanted to keep her vow.

"Anne! No, don't be sorry," she says. "Just think what would have happened to you if you had drunk all of it."

"That's true."

"Anne," she says in a very low voice, "you could have died."

"What the hell is a coach doing bringing around a guy like that?!" My face is starting to feel hot from anger. My fear and confusion have now turned to outrage. "The coach laughed when his friend handed me the drink; he must have known." I'm starting to remember everything up until the moment after taking the shot. At that point Eddie picked up a cup from the table, or maybe he pulled it out from behind his back . . . I'm struggling to remember exactly where it came from—but I do remember Terrance laughing when his friend said that he had "pussed out." The coach must have known.

the drugging

"Anne, why would he do that? He's a coach."

"Yeah, it's weird, but he laughed. He must have known."

"I don't know, Anne, but that's messed up—bringing drugs around kids."

"Yeah, I feel so bad for Cruz; he was really mad this morning. You know how he hates alcohol." Cruz's cousin was hit by a drunk driver five years ago; although she survived after months of therapy, we have all been cautious with alcohol around the kids.

"I'm sorry; if I hadn't been so out of it I could have helped calm him down."

"It's okay—you were drugged, too."

"Now it makes sense; I couldn't find the words to comfort him last night. I know I could have if I hadn't been so out of it."

I start to think . . . I was drugged. I fell all over the house, I threw up—but how did I end up in my bed? "Rhonda, how did I end up in bed? I woke up this morning in bed."

"Your assistant coach Ken was helping you in the bathroom. He went in there when you were throwing up. That's what made Cruz start to cry—he was trying to get into the bathroom but we wouldn't let him."

"He was in the bathroom with me, alone?" My heart drops. *Oh God—what if something happened in the bathroom? Could he have drugged me?* I'm confused and scared; my heart starts to race again.

"He didn't do anything to you, Anne," she says in a comforting voice. "We were right outside the door."

"I'm relieved. "I hope I didn't say anything to him or try to kiss him!!" I've always thought he was hot—and he is so sweet. He doesn't wear a wedding ring, so for the first few weeks I thought he was single. I may have had a little crush on him. Now I'm embarrassed, not because I threw up in front of him but because I might have tried to kiss him—and gosh, with vomit breath!

"I hope not; you were throwing up in the toilet!" she laughs. "That would be gross!"

I laugh with ease and start to feel a little better. I end the phone call, telling her I'm going to go down to the local urgent care and get tested for GHB. It's a drug that is otherwise known as a roofy; it was well known back in the nineties as a date-rape drug. It's illegal in most countries and is very dangerous because it's mixed with acid, so it's been known to kill.

I lie back on the bed and stare at the ceiling. I start to cry. How could I have let this happen to me? *God, why did you let this happen?* Cruz is so hurt and scared now—I let him down. My emotions are uncontrollable; my body is shaking and the tears don't stop.

I sit up and pray. "Please give me peace right now. I'm scared and don't know what to do . . . Cruz doesn't trust me, and I let him down." Suddenly I feel a sense of peace come over me. I feel that God is telling me that I'll be all right and to reassess the situation.

Still feeling drugged I get up and throw some grey sweats on and a large black t-shirt. I put my hair up and look at my face. *Yikes.* Oh well—I don't care how I look right now. I need to get to Urgent Care before it closes.

On arrival, I open the door and look around. Good—nobody is in the waiting room; I should be seen soon. I check in with the receptionist and sit down. Five minutes later my name is called by a lady with grey hair up in a bun, and wearing a long white nurse's gown. She ushers me in, takes my weight, and puts me in a waiting room.

"Doctor will be right with you," she says and walks out. Ten minutes later a doctor comes in and I explain to him what happened. He asks if I want to have a rape kit done, which I hadn't thought of before.

"No, that's ok. I think I would know if I was raped; it's been a while since I've had sex." He seems hesitant to let me slide on the rape kit, but finally agrees to have a urine test and blood work.

The nurse comes back in and takes some of my blood and hands me a plastic cup with a blue lid. "Please urinate into this."

I walk down the hall into the bathroom, feeling like a zombie, walking around in a dreamlike state. I can't believe this happened to me. Coming out of the bathroom, I hand the nurse my urine sample. Still in a daze, I enter back into the room and sit on the chair. It seems like forever before they come back.

"Anne," the doctor says, opening the door. "I have bad news for you." He looks down at his file. "You were drugged; your test came back positive for GHB."

"Oh my gosh, I knew it." I feel somewhat relieved, but now I'm angry again. I take a deep breath to calm down.

"Now, I'm not sure what exactly you were drugged with," he says, putting his hand on my shoulder. "We will send it out to a lab for more results—should come back in five to seven days."

"Wow." I start to cry.

"You will be okay; you've made it through the worst part," he says. "It might take up to a week for you to get all of your senses back, though; these drugs do a number on the brain."

"Good—. I won't be like this forever??"

"You'll start feeling better in a few days."

I leave Urgent Care and head home to go back to bed, but just before lying down, I respond to Toby's text. He had texted me yesterday about the barbeque, but I had forgotten to respond, so I apologize for having missed it.

The next morning I wake up and force myself to go to church. I don't like missing church unless I am out of town; no matter how I'm feeling, church always puts me in a better mood.

After church I go back home to get some work done, but I can't get myself to concentrate on anything. I give up and turn on the TV; the Angels and Dodgers are playing. I cuddle up with a soft blanket and text Rhonda. I haven't talked to her since last night and want her to know I had been drugged. She tells me I should call the police, but I don't want some creep coming after me because I turned him in. It's hard enough living on my own, but I'm not about to put Cruz at risk, too. After some texting back and forth, I fall asleep to the sound of the baseball game.

I wake up to my phone ringing. It's Cruz. "Hey, bud."

"Hi, Mom. Are you feeling better?"

"Yes, honey. I'm feeling a lot better." I look at the clock: six o'clock. "You know how there are bad people out there that will do bad things to others?"

"Yeah," he responds, curiously.

"Well, somebody did something bad to me. I was drugged on Friday night."

"Drugged?" he asks. "What does that mean?"

"I went to the hospital yesterday and they tested me for drugs. Unfortunately, there are bad people in the world who will put a drug into someone's drink and walk away."

"Who drugged you?" He sounds worried.

"I'm not sure. I guess someone at the pool."

"It was the coach's friend!" he yells. "He looked like a guy that would be on the run from the cops."

"I don't know, honey," I laugh. "We can't judge people by their looks."

"Mom, you have to promise me that you will never drink again."

"Honey, I can't promise you I'll never drink again, but I will promise that I won't drink around you for a long time—and I can promise that I will be extremely careful when drinking around strangers."

"But Mom—"

"Deal?"

"Ok, Mom—. Deal."

We talk a little bit longer, and with every word I can hear the anxiety from the previous night slowly disappearing from his voice. I end the phone call with lots of "I love you's" and kisses.

The work week flies by. It's not until five days later that I recover most of my senses, and it almost feels as if nothing had ever happened. I've moved all the alcohol into locked cabinets, and Cruz seems to have forgotten about the drugging—that, or he's just not talking about it.

As I'm dropping him off at his dad's house the following weekend, I see his half-brother Jay walking out the door with his head down. "Hi, Jay," I say as I nudge his shoulder to get his attention.

"Oh, hey, Anne." He stops and gives me a hug.

"How've you been? Ready for school to be over?"

"Yeah—five more weeks."

"That's great! Let me know when graduation is, okay?"

"Sure. Hey—did you ever make that trip to Indonesia?"

"Huh? You mean Costa Rica?"

"No, Indonesia," he replies. "Thought you went to Indonesia."

"Nope, I didn't go to Indonesia, but I went to Costa Rica and it was really cool."

"Yeah, I heard it has some of the best surfing." He gives me another hug and tells me he has to go.

I walk Cruz up to his dad's house and give him a kiss and hug. "See you next week, bud. Love you."

"I love you, too, Mom." He hugs me back. "I'm going to miss you." He starts to cry.

"It's only five days, bud. I'll call you every day."

"Okay." He gives me another hug and steps into the house.

That night Rhonda and I decide to chill. We meet up at the gym, and afterwards grab some sushi. We both make a pact that we'll watch out for each other and never leave each other alone while drinking.

*********

Although I haven't opened my eyes yet, I can feel the sun's rays on my face. I turn over in bed trying to avoid waking up, but it doesn't work. I open my eyes, sit up, and look at the clock. It's early. Lying back down, I cover my face with a pillow. It's Saturday morning, and I should take advantage of being able to sleep in. My mind starts to race with things I should do, one of which should be the gym.

I get out of bed and make my way downstairs. The sun is blazing through the house; it's going to be a beautiful day. I stand at the balcony looking out the windows thinking how blessed I am to be living here. On clear days I can see Catalina Island. Turning into the kitchen, I make myself a protein shake with fresh strawberries and bananas; this should be a good pick-me-up for the gym.

That night I stay in to relax on the couch with a good book. This past week has taken a toll on my mind, body, and soul. It's times like this that I realize I don't do enough of it. I find myself constantly busy with work and friends that I starve myself of much-needed attention to the soul. Everyone needs time to reflect. It was my older sister who told me soon after my divorce to slow down and focus on me. Being a twin, I had always surrounded myself with people. From birth, I had always been attached to someone, never learning to be alone. After my divorce, I focused on being alone—but most importantly, knowing that it's okay to be alone. I had a dependence on others for my happiness. Growing up, I thought that as long as my twin sister or a friend was around, then I should be happy—but in time I learned that happiness needs to come from within, not from others. If we allow others to dictate our happiness, then we are merely slaves to others.

# God's calling

For the last several Sundays I have been taking my friend Ivy to church with me. She's been going through a nasty divorce and needs spiritual guidance. She was raised with a strong Christian faith but strayed during her marriage, spending more time on her kids than on her relationship with God. Life happens; we all get busy and unfortunately set God aside—until we need Him.

As Ivy and I walk into church, I grab the weekly bulletin. It has the basic church information with service times and contact details, but it also consists of an insert that includes the weekly message and upcoming events.

We sit down just as the service begins. Today it is about living our life for God. As the pastor concludes the service in singing, I flip the bulletin over to see what is happening this week. Along the right side of the bulletin it reads: **Upcoming Global Connection Trips** in bold, and below it: *Information meetings for Iraq and Indonesia happening soon! If you're interested in joining either of these trips, check out the information sessions this week: Indonesia Session: March third at 1 p.m. For Iraq Session: March 6 at 6 p.m.*

*Wow—that's weird*, I think to myself. *Indonesia—didn't Jay just ask me about Indonesia?* I pick up my phone and snap a quick picture of the bulletin. I have to attend this Indonesia meeting this week—seems like more than a coincidence.

I point to the bulletin and look at Ivy. "I think I might look into this. I'm not sure why, but I feel like I need to attend this." I remember that I have friends who moved to Bali a couple years ago; it would also be nice to see them.

As we walk out of church, I look at my phone to see the picture I took of the bulletin. I don't want to miss the meeting. It then dawns on me that the meeting is today! I look at the meeting time again; it's at one o'clock—and it's almost one now! I tell Ivy, who asks me to drop her off at home first.

It is exactly one o'clock as I pull into the parking lot. I ask church staff for the meeting location, and an older man points in the direction of the café.

With a fast pace, I walk in and look around. A group of people are standing around a short, stalky man holding a paper. "Do you know where the meeting is for the Indonesia trip?"

He looks down at his paper and then back up at me. "What's your name?"

"Anne Latour. Is this the group that's meeting for the Indonesia missions trip?"

"Yes. Have you filled out an application yet?" he asks.

"Umm, no . . ." I pause, confused. "I saw that you guys were having an information meeting on the trip, so I thought I'd come check it out."

"Okay. No worries. It's not too late to join; everyone here has already filled out the application, but if you decide to go, then you can do it online."

I follow everyone upstairs. The church built this new building a couple years ago, and I had never really taken the time to check it out. The hallways are painted in a calm but bright, neutral color, along with deep browns and reds. I like it. We all sit down in the conference room around a large wooden oval table. Everything smells new. The back wall of the conference room consists of huge windows overlooking the church common area. I sit down next to the man who seems to be in charge. Everyone else in the room seems to be much younger than me, probably in their twenties.

The man stands up next to me. "Hello, everyone! I'm Doug, and I will be leading this trip to Indonesia. I've been on a couple global trips with the church, once to Africa and once to Indonesia. The trip we do to Indonesia is laid back, perfect for those of you who have never been on a global trip. Why don't we start by going around the room, telling a little bit about yourself and why you're going on the trip?"

Everyone stands up—mostly college students—and they start to talk about who they are and why they're going. The consensus seems to be for surfing. One slightly overweight lady in the back of the room says she wants to go because she has always wanted to visit Indonesia. She sits back down and rocks an odd-looking stroller next to her. As someone else stands to talk, a bark comes from the stroller. She pulls back the blanket draped over the front and lifts up a very small Chihuahua. "Quiet, Petey," she says, snuggling it to her large chest.

I hold back the laughter and put my head down. Doug leans into the table. "Excuse me, but would you like to take your dog outside? We can wait a couple minutes before continuing."

The lady puts the dog back inside the stroller and stands up. "I think I am going to leave now. It's not fair for Petey to be cooped up in here." She pushes the stroller out, and shuts the door just when I am ready to burst out with laughter.

They continue around the room, talking about themselves and why they are going. Then it's my turn. I stand up.

"My name is Anne Latour. I don't know if I am going on this trip; I just read about it today. I'm here to hear more about it; but I've always been interested in going on a mission trip. I'm thirty-six years old, I have a nine-year-old son, and I run an accounting business." I sit back down and see that I'm the last person to speak.

Doug stands up and explains that they'll be gone for two weeks in late May, traveling to a small and remote island in Indonesia. The mission is to stay with villagers, displaying Christian behavior. The island is predominantly Muslim, and their only insight into Western society is what's on TV: *Jersey Shore*, *Baywatch*, and other scandalizing programs.

Although Indonesia's constitution guarantees freedom of religion, the country is comprised mostly of Muslims and Hindus… If Christians went onto the island handing out bibles and building churches, they would be run out—and not in a friendly way, either. It takes years to establish a connection with the people, so the church will send in a team to mix with them under the guise of being tourists. This is a perfect introduction to missions work, because there won't be too much "work" being done, except in the team's behavior, exhibiting good Christian values among the people. Everyone has to be in shape because we will be hiking, surfing, snorkeling, and so forth. I think back to the overweight lady with the dog; there's no way she would be able to go on this trip—and she probably would have wanted to bring her pet. I shake off the laughter and feel a sense of togetherness with the group. This could be a perfect trip for me. I am good with people and I am in shape; sleeping on floors and eating strange food won't bother me.

Doug concludes the meeting with prayer, asking everyone to go around the table adding their own prayer. As it comes to me, I say, "Dear God, I pray that You lead me to make the right decision whether or not to go on this trip. I ask that You give me peace with my decision and that no matter what the outcome You keep everyone safe and prepare our hearts for what is to come." The prayer concludes and I shake Doug's hand. "I'll let you know my decision by the end of the week."

"Okay, thanks. The application is on the church website. There's a five hundred dollar deposit due with the app."

As I walk to my car, a wave of excitement comes over me. I feel like God wants me to go on this trip. I've never felt this way before. I feel excited and yet at peace with the thought of leaving Cruz and my business for two weeks. I get in the car and dial my mom.

"Hi, Anne," she answers with a cheery voice. I don't call her often, so when I do, it makes her happy.

"Mom! You would not believe what I might do! I think I might go to Indonesia with my church—on a missions trip." I am still sitting in my car in the parking lot.

"Indonesia?"

"Yes! Mom, it's weird, but I feel like God wants me to go," I continue. I explain to her about Jay and how he had asked me how my visit to Indonesia had been, when I had never actually gone, and then the strange coincidence of the meeting listed in the church bulletin.

"Wow, Anne—that sounds crazy. I think you should take time to pray about it."

"Yeah, I will. I have no idea how I would be able to leave Cruz for two weeks. And Mom, I can't just leave the country; my clients depend on me every day."

"Anne, if this is what God wants, He will provide. Everything will work out."

"True," I say, turning my car on. I can't believe I am thinking about going to Indonesia. This is crazy.

"Pray about it. I'll be praying for you to make the right decision."

"Thanks, Mom. I gotta' go." I pull out of the church parking lot. "I'll call you later."

We hang up and I say a prayer. *God, if this is what you want from me, please make it known.*

Later that day I call Rhonda to tell her about the trip. She doesn't seem too happy about it. She's never been outside of the United States and thinks it's dangerous to do so. I explain that it would be safe for us because we won't be Bible thumping; we'll be tourists, and the villagers would be disgraced if something were to happen to us. I assure her the church went before and nothing happened.

That night I sit on my bed with my Bible and pray about my decision. All day I have felt that God wants me to go on the trip, but a part of me wonders if I'm getting a mixed feeling because the idea of leaving the country sounds exciting. I ask God to give me peace about the decision and to give me a clear answer. Not only is there a decision to make, I would have to raise three thousand dollars, tell Cruz I'd be gone for two weeks, and figure something out with my clients—not to mention save money for the hours I would not be billing them. First things first: I need to figure out if God wants me to go.

The next few days are spent meditating in prayer. I pick Cruz up one afternoon and want to be able to discuss it with him. I have a feeling he will take it badly and will tell me not to go, but it's only fair of me to include him in my decision process. Up to this point, I have continued to feel that God wants me to go, but maybe my discussion with Cruz will lead me in another direction.

As I drive to the school to pick him up, I pray again: *God, please give me the right words to say to Cruz; please give him the peace and understanding to know that this would be for you.* I pull up to the school and see Cruz standing next to his friends talking and laughing. He looks up at me, says good-bye to his friends, and runs up to the car.

"Hi, Mom," he says, getting into the car with a big smile. "I don't have any homework today."

"Awesome, bud," I respond, and give him a hug.

We drive along the road for several moments in silence; it's as if he knows I want to say something. Cruz has always been in tune with me. It's a good thing, but also a drawback because I can't hide anything from him.

"Bud," I say to break the silence.

"Yeah, Mom?"

"Ummm . . ." I'm a little nervous, yet excited. "You know how I told you to pray about your decision to go on that overnight class trip?"

"Yep, Mom—and it worked," he said with a smile. "I had so much fun on that trip. When can I do it again?"

Earlier in the year Cruz's class had gone on an overnight trip to learn about a Mission in San Diego, but since Cruz had never slept away from home before, he had been scared about going. We prayed every day and every night about his decision, and by the time he was ready to leave for the trip, he felt comfortable knowing God wanted him to go. It was a great opportunity for me to teach him how to lean on God when faced with a decision.

"I think God wants me to go to Indonesia."

He turns to me with huge eyes. "Indonesia? Isn't that on the other side of the world?"

"Yes, honey," I say, grabbing his hand. "I feel that God wants me to go there, to spread the Word—to teach others about Him."

"Who would you go with?"

"The church; they're putting together a group of people to go in May."

"That's next month, Mom!"

"Honey, I've been praying about this and truly feel that God wants me to go. I have never felt so sure about something as I do this."

He tightens his grip around my hand and looks up at me. "Mom, if God wants you to go . . . then you have to go."

Tears well up in my eyes. I take a deep breath. "Ok, bud. Thanks for your encouragement." This is it; this is truly a sign from God. It's almost a miracle how well he takes the news.

"How long will you be gone?"

"Probably two weeks."

"That's a long time, Mom!" I can see the wheels turning in his head; the thought of being away from me for so long has got to be scary. "Who will I stay with?"

"Your dad." I'd rather my mom come down and spend time with him while I'm gone, but knowing my ex-husband, he wouldn't allow that, and he has the first right of refusal since it's going to be more than twenty-four hours.

"Will I be able to call you every night?"

"No, honey. I'm sorry, but it's in a different time zone and I might not have reception—but I will try to call you as often as possible and I can send you emails. Okay?"

"Okay, Mom."

We pull into the garage. I feel like a huge weight has been lifted off of my shoulders knowing Cruz is ok with my leaving. It makes everything else seem so easy. Next, I need to fill out the paper work and start fundraising.

That night I email the paper work to the church and create my letter to send out to all my friends, family, and clients. Although the church has a standardized letter to send out, I feel compelled to create a personalized letter explaining how I felt called to go and why. The church wants me to raise three thousand dollars for this trip, which would be hard to do without reaching out to everyone I know—some of whom will think I'm absolutely crazy, especially going into a predominantly Muslim country. I am sure to add in my letter that the church has done the same trip in the past and that everyone was safe.

First thing in the morning, I check my emails to see if anyone has responded yet: four responses—and they all say they will be sending money to the church. They wish me luck and ask to be placed on my supporting prayer team. The church had asked that each one of us going create a prayer team led by someone who will be in the United States while we travel through Indonesia. I plan on asking Bridget later today. She has always been an inspiration to me; in fact, she is the one who led me to go to this church just after my divorce. She is organized, dependable, but most importantly, a strong Christian.

I spend most of the day calling my mom and close friends to tell them personally of my decision. My mom is ecstatic, telling me that God will provide and that everything will work out. Bridget agrees to be my prayer team leader and asks if she can also support in a financial way. What a blessing! Everyone seems to want to help me out in one way or another. God truly is amazing; He can work in such mysterious ways.

**********

By the end of the second week, I have raised three times the amount needed. Since I joined the team late, I had been worried I wouldn't have enough time to raise the money—yet I raised three times as much! To make it more obvious that God wants me to go, I receive a phone call from a client asking me to work on a project for him with a deadline the same week I'll be leaving for Indonesia. Timing couldn't be more perfect. Although the job would require up to eighteen-hour days, I accept it, knowing this will be a good opportunity to save money for the time I'll be gone.

Everything is coming together smoothly—but there is one last person to tell: Dave. The last time we spoke, it was just after I'd been drugged. He had come over to bring food and cuddle with me. I know he'll be supportive of my decision to go; he is somewhat spiritual as well and travels around the world for business, so he won't be scared for me like other friends have been. My only hesitation is that I will also be telling him that we need to stop being intimate. Over these past couple weeks, I have felt that God wants me to be pure, especially before going on this missions trip—no alcohol and no sex. I know it will be hard because every time I see Dave, one thing leads to another, and then he leaves to go back to his busy life. Although I have felt okay with it in the past and have accepted that he could never commit to me, the transformation I've undergone since my decision to go to Indonesia has led me to see things in a different light. I believe God wants more from me, and I'm unable to give that to Him while living a promiscuous life. I keep asking God to bring me a man who has time for me, and yet I keep spending time with a man who doesn't. Maybe this trip and this dedication to be pure is a step in the right direction, a step closer to God and a step further away from my unhealthy relationship with Dave.

I pick up my phone and dial him, leaving a voice message asking if he wants to do dinner. I don't have Cruz back until early next week and want to take advantage of this opportunity to talk. Typically Dave doesn't respond to my messages for a day or two, but knowing my schedule, I hope he'll get back to me quickly.

I spend the rest of the day working. This new project has taken up a lot of my time, leaving me very little time for the gym or hanging out with friends. I guess this is another God thing in disguise, as it has made it easier to stay away from alcohol.

In the early evening, Dave calls to say he can come by around nine o'clock after work. I tell him I'll make a late dinner. I then run to the market; I haven't had time to cook let alone shop. I have nothing in the house to make dinner with.

*********

Just as I finish sautéing the vegetables, Dave calls from the front gate. I rush around the house, straightening things up, lighting candles, and strategically placing my Indonesia information packet on the coffee table. As I head down stairs to open the door for him, I stop to say a prayer. *God, please give me the right words to say and the strength to end this with Dave tonight.* I open the door.

"Hi, Miss." We hug.

"Hi! Good to see you."

"Sorry, I've been really busy."

"It's all good—me, too." He has no idea how busy I have been.

We walk upstairs and he turns Sports Center on as I serve dinner. We eat in front of the TV with some small talk. I want to wait until after the dishes are cleared to tell him about the trip and about my decision to be pure.

*35*

As I clear the last plate from the coffee table, I start to talk from the kitchen. "I've decided to go on a church missions trip—to Indonesia. It's a strange story, but I really feel like God wants me to go."

"That's cool, Anne," he responds nonchalantly. "Good for you."

I explain to him about the curious remarks from my ex-stepson, and then the coincidental meeting about Indonesia at my church, and how everything seems to have fallen into place.

"That's incredible," he responds. "What are you going to do about Cruz?"

"He's going to stay with his dad," I shrug. He knows I don't like leaving Cruz with his dad too long. "You know what's weird, though, is that when I told Cruz, he was okay with my leaving."

"Really?" He looks at me with eyebrows raised.

"Yes, it's another sign from God. I've never felt so right about anything; it's scary to be taking this leap of faith, traveling to a country known to persecute Christians—and yet I know God wants me to go."

"You'll be okay, Miss." He pulls me close and wraps his arms around me. I always feel so safe with him; if only I could count on him to always be here for me. Every time we're together I feel like we can conquer the world—but when he leaves, I feel so empty. Love shouldn't feel this way.

"You're such a good person, Anne." He pulls my chin up, looking into my eyes. He leans down and kisses me; his soft lips on mine make me forget why he's here. I pull back, but he grabs the back of my head gently and pulls me back in. *Oh God, please help me be strong.* He kisses me so sensually it's hard to think about anything but ripping his clothes off and ravishing him.

"Dave . . ." I start to say.

"Come on," he says pulling me up off the couch, "Let's go to bed."

We walk upstairs. *God, please—please help me be strong and tell him we can't do this anymore . . . God, please give me the will power and strength.*

These past several years, I have tried to end the sexual side of our relationship, but it always ends in the bed. We have had such a strong connection, which makes it hard to end the physical part; plus, we've been together so long that we know how to please each other. It's crazy how long we've been with each other and yet still with such chemistry. I think that this is exactly what I want with my husband.

Dave's ahead of me as we walk up the stairs, and just as he gets into my bedroom, he turns and pulls me into his arms. We stand there hugging for what seems like hours but in reality only several minutes. He kisses me on the top of my head "I am so proud of you, Anne," he smiles. "You are going to do big things in life."

He traces my lips with his finger and then leans down to kiss my cheek. *Thank God*, I think to myself. But it doesn't end there. His fingers run down my chin, down my neck, and then across my breast, ending at the bottom of my shirt. He slowly pulls it up over my head and starts to kiss my neck, while pushing me onto the bed. My body loves every second of this, but my mind is screaming: *No! Don't do this, Anne!* I pull him up and barely squeak out the words, "No, I don't think this is a good idea."

He shushes me and continues.

"Noooooo," I whisper again. He always feels so good and my body really wants him, but it can't happen. I sit up and turn over, facing him. "I don't think we should do this. You've made it clear to me you can't commit."

"I thought we talked about this before and you were okay with the way things are." He sits up and looks at me with his beautiful eyes. "You know how I feel about you. I love you, but I'm not in the same place as you. I don't know if I ever will be."

"Exactly, Dave. I can't keep doing this." I grab a pillow and prop it up under my elbows. "God keeps telling me that he has a man for me, but I need to end this, end us. Who knows—maybe it's you. I just know that God doesn't want me in an open relationship. I need to be in a committed relationship, with someone who's not just sleeping with me."

"I'm sorry, too." I hold onto him. I don't want to forget this feeling, being in his arms. He pulls me tighter, kisses me on the forehead, and whispers in my ear, "One last time. Let's have one last night.

# preparations

The next morning I wake up cuddled against Dave with his arms around me. I slowly slide out from under his grasp and get out of bed. What have I done? I wasn't supposed to have sex with him. *Damn.* This has to be my last time. *God, I promise you—this is it. I will not have sex with him anymore. Please forgive me.* I take a shower to wash all the guilt off; surprisingly I feel much better when I step out. Dave is already dressed and sitting on the bed.

"I have an eight o'clock phone call," he says, standing up. He walks over to me and kisses me on the lips. "I'll call you later. I have an unlocked blackberry to give you for your trip; you'll be able to use it in Indonesia."

"Thank you." I give him a hug. "About last night—"

He puts his finger to my lips. "I know; it was the last time."

He kisses me on the cheek and leaves.

**********

That day, all I could think about was our night, the way he touched my body, the way we moved as one. How could God find a more perfect man for me?

I am so sidetracked that I completely forget that my missions team has a meeting at seven o'clock. I look at my watch and it is ten till seven; the day has flown by. Tonight we will be going over the logistics, what to wear, how to act; we might even Skype with the family we'll be visiting.

I grab a bottle of water from the fridge and throw on a light jacket. I pull up to the house, which belongs to the parents of the man who lives in Indonesia. As I walk in, I realize I'm a little late and that everyone has been sitting there waiting for me.

I apologize, sitting down next to a woman not much older than me.

"No problem. We were just talking about the bathroom situation in Indonesia." He adjusts in his chair. We are all sitting in a large great room connected to the kitchen.

"So," he goes on to say, "the bathrooms—well, there really aren't any." He laughs uneasily. "Have you ever heard of a squatty potty?" A few people giggle. "They are holes in the ground with a piece of wood on each side to keep your feet on. For women the term is certainly squat because there is nothing to sit on." Everyone laughs.

I raise my hand. "Can we use toilet paper?" More laughs.

"Yes. In fact we'll give everyone a roll of toilet paper when we get there."

I'm thinking, heck no—I'll bring my own roll of Charmin. If I'm going to rough it, I'm going to at least have a choice in how I rough it.

"Besides the bathroom situation, there is something else we have to talk about." Doug's looking serious now. "We will be swimming, and for those of you who want to, we'll be surfing." He looks at a couple of the guys as if they've already talked about it. "There will be a dress code. For us guys it's not a problem, but for most of you ladies, it might be."

I sit up straighter now. He goes on to say, "You cannot wear bikinis; you must wear board shorts no shorter than the knee and a rash guard with long sleeves. In fact, the guys need to wear a long-sleeved rash guard, too. The sun can be intense and after hours on the water, the skin will burn."

All of us girls look at one another. I blurt out, "I guess I won't be getting a tan there." They all laugh. I'm already thinking to myself that I'll have to do a day shopping trip downtown to pick up some boy board shorts and a sexy rash guard. Just because I have to cover up doesn't mean I can't be cute.

We end the meeting with a phone call to Jared and Jamie, the couple that currently lives in Indonesia. He tells us the weather has been hot and to bring lots of sunblock; he also says we might be able to attend a wedding while there. I love culture and learning about other people's traditions; this is going to be so exciting!

I call my mom on the way home to tell her about the meeting. Now I have a huge shopping list of things I need to buy, like a head lamp because there is no electricity, and plenty of long-sleeved clothing along with skirts because we aren't allowed to show our legs. I will also need to buy a back pack big enough to fit everything because we are only allowed to bring what we can carry; and we will be sleeping on the ground, so I'll need to buy a self-inflatable air mattress. This sure is going to be an expensive trip.

I spend the next few days shopping and working on finishing up my client's project. It was difficult to find a back pack large enough to fit everything I need for the trip, yet small enough to squeeze into the airplane overhead cabinet. I also ended up purchasing a cute outfit for surfing at a local surf shop. Tonight I have my last team meeting before we leave on the trip. Everything is starting to come together.

The team meeting goes well. We take a personality test and discuss our differences in leadership and team building skills. The test results show that I am an extrovert, sensational, a thinker and judger. That would make me practical, realistic, matter of fact, with a natural head for business or mechanics. It also shows that I am not interested in abstract theories and that I want what I learn to have a direct or immediate application. I like to organize and run activities. I would make a good administrator, as I am decisive and quickly move to implement decisions, taking care of routine details.

I am a little concerned about Doug's leadership role with the team, though; he doesn't seem sufficiently confident. He is a really nice guy, and I can see that he has a big heart, but he doesn't seem like a leader. I sense that I need to step up my game and be more alert on this trip. Thankfully, I have friends that live in Bali, so if anything goes wrong, I can call on them.

My friends in Bali are a married couple I met several years ago in the United States. We met through mutual friends and have been close ever since. They have two boys the same age as Cruz, so it was nice getting together and letting the boys play, but now they are so far away and the only time we can catch up is through Facebook. I am excited to spend some time with them when I go to Indonesia; the church told me we'll have a couple days in Bali on the way back to the United States.

The meeting ends shortly after our discussion and another Skype call to Jared and Jamie. When I get home, I make myself some chamomile tea and sit down on the couch with my Bible. I've been spending every day and night meditating on God's Word. I have never felt closer to God than I have these past weeks since making my commitment to go on this trip. I have been having conversations with God for years now, but this just makes it more real, almost as if I've confirmed that I have been really talking to God all these years.

I first started talking to God just after my divorce. It was the hardest time in my life. Both my parents were married for over thirty years, and all their parents before that. I married to be married for a lifetime, so when I felt that God was telling me that it was okay to leave my ex-husband, it was the hardest decision I'd ever made.

One night after a long day in court, I was sitting on my bed praying and crying, when all of a sudden I heard a voice in my head. It sounded like my voice, almost as if I were talking to myself, but the difference was that I felt a wave of calmness come over me. I stopped crying and felt as if everything would be okay; it was weird, because I had gone from complete hysteria to complete relaxation. The voice told me that everything would be okay, and that I needed to trust Him. From that day forward, I had conversations with God. Some days, I didn't feel His presence—usually during the times I wasn't focusing on Him. There were times after I had stopped talking to Him for weeks at a time that it would take me an hour just sitting quietly to get focused back on Him enough to hear His voice. I would sit on my bed praying to clear my mind, body, and soul of all negative things, waiting to hear God's voice. Up until being called by God to go on this trip, I had always wondered if I really was talking to God, or if I was talking to myself. I know it's crazy, because we are supposed to have faith in God, like the Scripture verse in Hebrews 11:1 says: "Faith is being sure of what we hope for and certain of what we do not see." Now that I have seen actual signs from God that He wants me to go on this trip, I am certain this is the path I am to follow; it confirms everything I've been doing since my divorce.

As I am praying and meditating on God's Word, I pray that the trip is successful and that we all stay safe. Lately there have been stories in the news of Christians being persecuted in Muslim countries; although God wouldn't be sending us if it weren't part of a bigger picture, I am a bit scared that something might happen. Just as I bring my prayer to a close, I feel an overwhelming sense of anxiety. I don't get anxious much, if at all, so I sit for a while longer, praying for a sense of peace. I then hear God's voice. *Something will happen in Indonesia.* My heart starts to race and I feel really cold. The hairs on my arm start to rise. I ask, *What will happen?* He responds, *Something will happen, but you will be okay.* I continue, *God, please—I'm scared. What's going to happen?* At this point my heart is beating so loudly that I almost can't concentrate. God responds again, *Don't worry; everything will be okay.* I then feel a sense of calmness come over me and my heart stops racing. *Strange,* I think to myself; *I wonder what will happen . . .* God says it'll be okay, so I guess there's nothing to worry about. I close my Bible and finish my tea.

**********

Waking up with a ton of things to do is not always fun. I jump out of bed and take London out for a walk, meanwhile making a list in my head of all the things I need to accomplish today. First I need to drop off the completed project to my client and then pick up my prescriptions from the pharmacy. The church recommended bringing along an antibiotic just in case we pick up a viral infection.

When I travel, I pack the entire pharmacy. It's actually a joke among my friends—I am always prepared for the worst. Ten years ago, I went skiing with my ex-husband. We were at a mountain I had never skied before and I was a bit too confident. I took a jump on my skies and ended up crushing both my feet. I was in extreme pain until I got down the mountain to the emergency room. Ever since, I've told myself always to have pain killers on hand when doing dangerous activities. We will be surfing and hiking in another country, with who knows what kind of medical facilities. I will definitely pack some high-grade pain killers, along with other needed medicine.

As I get back to the house, I arrange for my friend's brother, who lives across the street, to watch London while I'm gone. He agrees to take care of her as long as I stock the fridge with beer. After a quick shower, I head to my client's office.

*43*

"Hi, Anne," the receptionist greets me when I walk through the door. "Are you all ready for your trip?"

"Just about, although I'm getting a little nervous."

"Don't be nervous—you're going for a good cause." "If you're looking for Guy, he's at lunch with a client." Guy has been a client of mine for a couple years now; he runs an accounting firm and has been a big part in the growth of my business.

"Okay. I just wanted to drop off all these files for him."

She takes them from me and sets them down on her desk. "I'll give them to Guy when he gets back." The files are complete and fairly easy to understand. He won't need to call me, but he'll probably want to wish me luck on my trip, though. He was also a big part of my financial contribution team, donating a large amount of money. I am blessed to have such amazing people in my life.

I head home and pick up my prescriptions from the pharmacy. I want to spend some one-on-one time with Cruz reflecting. I will be leaving the country to a possibly unsafe area, so who knows what could happen? Every so often I talk with Cruz about what would happen if I were to die. I know it's not a bright subject, but I worry about how he would take it. We are extremely close—I feel almost as close to him as I do my twin sister. Sometimes I think he can finish my sentences or know what I am thinking. It worries me how he would react if I were to die. I tell him I will always be with him deep in his heart, and that he can always pray through God to me. I also tell him how much I love him and that my love will never go away, even if I'm not on earth anymore. I think that so often when a child loses a parent, he feels so lonely; I know, because even as an adult when I lost my dad, I felt like a piece of me had died, too. Cruz is a bright kid with a lot of life ahead of him; I would hate to see him fall apart if something were to happen to me.

I pick Cruz up from school. He is surprised to see me so early, so I tell him that I just want some time with him before my trip. We stop by Dairy Queen for some ice cream and head to the beach.

"Mom, over here," Cruz says, running out on to the sand with his ice cream. The weather is perfect. The sun is shining and high in the sky; it feels almost like summer, even though it is only May. Spring can be hit or miss here in Southern California; sometimes it can be grey for days at a time, or sometimes it can be beautiful and warm like today.

I'm not a huge fan of ice cream, but Cruz loves it, so I eat it every once in a while, which is usually on the first and last day of school. It's a tradition I started with his step-brother years ago. Today is a different day, though; it's a time of reflection, not over the school year but over our life.

"Cruz, come back over here. I don't want to get my feet sandy!" I shout. He's kicking up the sand, laughing. I love how carefree he is and yet ever so cautious. He sits down next to me. "You haven't eaten much."

"No, I'm not very hungry." I smile at him. "Bud, I love you very much."

"I love you, too, Mom." He puts his little arm around my shoulders and squeezes. "I'm going to miss you."

"I will, too, bud, but we'll talk as often as I have a chance to, okay?"

"Okay." He's pushing his ice cream around in his bowl.

"I'll bring you back something from Indonesia, something different that other kids won't have here—and I'm sure I'll have a lot of stories to tell you."

"Okay, Mom."

"I'm not saying anything will happen, but I want you to know I will always be with you—okay? I will always be in your heart. You don't have to look far—just dig deep in your heart and pray. You always have to remember to pray, okay, honey?" My eyes are welling with tears, so I have to look away.

"Mom! Nothing will happen to you."

"I know, bud, but I just want you to know how much I love you."

"I love you, too, Mom."

We head back home just as the sun starts to set. I make his favorite dinner, macadamia nut-encrusted halibut. That night I don't do anything but snuggle with him. This is our last night until I leave for my trip—I want to cherish every moment of it.

*Bali Girl*

**\*\*\*\*\*\*\*\*\***

The next several days leading up to our flight I spend with Rhonda. Although I am not drinking, I still go to the bars with her and chat. It's amazing how things look different when I am not drinking. Even men look less appealing. I make a note to myself to be more careful in my choice of men when I get back and start drinking again. Rhonda and I spend time talking about God and religion. I can see that it bothers her when I bring it up, but I don't care about discussing much else, as I feel so spiritual during this time. Rhonda was raised Jewish but isn't practicing anymore. She drinks a lot and dresses provocatively. Although she has a good heart, I think she has a lot of soul searching to do. I always wonder if God brought us together so that I can witness to her.

The night before my flight, Dave comes over to bring the unlocked Blackberry. He says I'll be able to use it in parts of the country where my iPhone phone won't work. It's times like this that confuse me, because it is clear he wants to protect me and provide for me—but he wants it on his own terms, in his own time.

We are sitting on the couch watching TV when he reaches over to pull me closer. I snuggle up closer to him. I have felt scared about my trip these past couple of days, so being in his arms feels good right now. I just need to make sure we don't do anything I will regret.

"Are you all packed?" He looks down at me.

"Yes, just about. Viviane, my team partner, is coming over in the morning to put together a shared suitcase with me. I just found out that besides our back pack, we can share one suitcase with our partner. We have to put our sleeping bag and air mattress in it, but I think we'll have some extra room for other things. I'm packing a lot of Clif Bars just in case I don't like the food over there." We both laugh. The church told us to partner up because we'd be sharing a suitcase and a hotel room on the way over there and the way back. Viviane is the older woman I sat next to during the second meeting. She's a blonde like me and very practical; I think we'll get along great.

46

preparations

"I'm sure you'll be fine. It's a lot of rice and probably fish." He then adds, "Do you mind if I stay here tonight? It's getting kind of late and I have an early morning."

"Umm, I guess." As much as I want to say no, I don't want to be alone on my last night.

"I could sleep on the couch," he says, sitting up.

"No, that's okay. You can sleep in the room with me—just promise to be good."

He laughs. "You're the one who has to be good. Every time something happens, it is when you're not being good." He is kind of right; I usually end up kissing him and then it leads to more—although last time, it was all him.

As I walk upstairs with him, I say a prayer. *God, please help us both to be good.* Last time we had sex, we both agreed it would be the last time—plus, I have been so focused on God that I don't think God would allow it to happen. Maybe there would be a divine intervention or something if we started getting hot and heavy.

I change into grey shorts and a black tank top while standing in my bathroom. As I come out, he is already in bed with the lights off. I rinse my mouth and get into bed. I snuggle up close to him as I always do, and he wraps his arm around me.

"I am so proud of you, Anne," he whispers into my ear.

"Thanks," I whisper back, nuzzling my head into the corner of his arm.

His body against mine is so warm and comforting. He must be reading my thoughts, because his hand starts to move down to my leg and then my bottom, and he's slowly moving his hand down my leg and back up. I can feel my heart beat increasing with each stroke. *Oh, God, no . . . not again.* He starts to kiss me on the back of my neck, my sweet spot. My skin crawls in a good way and my stomach flips. His hand is now at the end of my shorts and his fingers are reaching in. He starts to touch me as I try to tell him no, but I can't get the words out . . . His breath and kisses on the back of my neck are unbearable. I can't take it anymore; I turn over and start kissing him. *God, please forgive me, for I am about to sin.*

47

# travels to Indo

After he leaves the next morning, I sit in the middle of my bed and cry. *God, I am so sorry. I keep promising to you I will be good with Dave, and yet I never am. Why do I keep making the same mistakes over and over again? God, I promise when I come back from my trip, I will cut things off with Dave. I will use this trip to focus on You and clear my mind and my body of him.*

I want to be a new me when I return. I don't sit long enough to hear God's voice. I have a lot of things to get done today before I have to meet up with everyone at the church . . .

Viviane comes over just before lunch and we put together our bag. The bag will be checked in on the plane, so we are using a much larger bag. She has a lot of extras she's bringing for Jamie.

After she leaves, I take London out for a long run on the beach, stopping a few times to reflect on everything that has happened these past couple of months and where I am spiritually in my life. I am so grateful for all these wonderful things God has done. I am so blessed.

When I get back home, I set out all of London's care instructions on the counter. I typed up a couple of pages of instructions for Jack, indicating when he should feed her, how much exercise she needs, and who her veterinarian is. Jack is a good guy and has experience with pets, so I'm not worried.

Rhonda is coming over at six o'clock to take me to the church. We are all meeting there for prayers, and then they have a bus taking us to the airport. I am starting to get anxious, so I sit down and pray, which brings me peace. Amazing what the power of a quick prayer can do.

I realize I need to call my friend Carrie before I leave because we have a girls' weekend to Vegas planned the night I get back from Indonesia. We haven't spent much time together lately because she's started dating someone, but we've both set aside the weekend in Vegas to catch up.

"Hi, Anne!" Carrie answers cheerfully. I have never met anyone as positive and bright as she is. She is truly a role model for me. She is almost fifteen years older but we get along well. "Are you ready? You leave tonight, don't you?"

"Yes, our flight takes off at midnight; I'm so excited!" Just the sound of her voice lifts me up.

"I am excited for you! And I'm looking forward to our girls' trip when you get back!"

"Yeah—me, too. I will really need it! I'm already packed for Vegas." This will be quite a month of travel for me. I fly back into Los Angeles at midnight on a Thursday, and our flight to Las Vegas is scheduled for noon on Friday. "I don't think I'll even sleep Thursday night. I might as well stay on Indo time—that way I can party all night!" I laugh.

"Good idea!" she responds. "I will be praying for you."

"Thanks, Carrie. I love you."

"I love you, too. Stay safe, and we'll catch up when you get back."

I hang up the phone and sit on my couch. What a crazy month planned! I still can't believe this is happening—I am actually going across the world with a bunch of people I don't know. This will be good, though, and it's what God wants of me. I probably shouldn't have scheduled the Vegas trip; it might be a little much. Going from a Muslim country straight to sin city; I wonder if I'll be preaching to people in Vegas. I laugh out loud.

I carry my bags downstairs to the garage and pack up my phone chargers. Just then, Rhonda pulls up in her white SUV and helps me load everything in her car. "Do you think you have everything you'll need?" she asks as we get into her car.

I laugh, "God, I hope so!"

"Are you nervous?"

"I was earlier today, but I feel better now."

"I would be. I can't believe you are going. I'm scared for you." She looks like she's going to cry.

"Don't be, Rhonda. I'll be fine. Like I said, it's very safe and the villagers would be disgraced if something were to happen to us."

"Okay. If you say so."

As we pull up to the church we see a huge black limo van parked in the parking lot and a group of people standing around. Bags are being loaded in the back of the van and people are shuffling about. I get out and start loading my bags. There's a weird energy among everyone. Just as the last bag gets loaded, Doug calls everyone into a circle to pray. We stand there holding hands. One by one, someone says a prayer and it continues, ending back with Doug. I give Rhonda a hug and tell her I love her, and we both have tears in our eyes. "Let me know that you made it safely, ok?"

"I will, Rhonda." I give her one last hug and step into the van.

The door shuts and Doug yells out, "Ok, last chance to change your mind!" We all laugh. I take out my iPhone and text Cruz. *I'm on the way to the airport. I love you.*

Doug looks over at me and raises his eyebrows. "No phones."

There had been a small discussion about the use of phones while on the trip, but there never was a conclusive answer as to whether we could bring phones or not. Plus, I thought the rule was directed at my younger teammates.

"I brought it for pictures; I'm using it as my camera," I respond, smiling and holding it up. He has no idea that I also have the Blackberry Dave gave me. I will have to be discreet when I buy the SIM card in Bali.

We get to the airport and line up at the ticket counter. How exciting! I feel good energy and everyone seems positive. We don't know where we are sitting yet or even if we are sitting together. The church didn't make seat assignments, which I thought was weird but—oh, well!

We get our tickets and check the bags. I'll be sitting next to Neal. He's probably eighteen or nineteen years old but seems quite mature for his age. We all walk toward our gate, stopping along the way at different newsstands and snack shops. This will be our longest leg of the trip: fourteen hours long in coach. I had already set a schedule as to when I would eat, sleep, and watch movies. My neighbor Jack, who travels the world a lot, told me I won't be jet lagged if I prepare myself ahead of time by getting on their time zone.

Once we get on the plane, I ask the flight attendant to hold my meal until I ask for it. I know they'll be serving dinner once we get into the air but I'll be sleeping, so I don't want to miss out—plus, if I eat before taking my sleeping pill then it'll be harder for me to fall asleep. Neal is sitting to my right, Doug is behind me, with Viviane and the rest of the bunch behind us in the middle row, across from Doug and Viviane.

"Do you have things to do on the flight?" Neal asks me as he settles into his chair.

"Yeah, but I'll be sleeping most of the time." I show him my schedule and he laughs.

"You have it all scheduled out? What if you can't fall asleep?"

"I brought Ambien," I respond, laughing. "I cut them up into portions, so I can sleep in increments of time."

"Oh, okay."

I lean over into my bag and take out my UNO cards. "You want to play?"

"Sweet! Yeah."

We play for an hour until it's time for me to take my Ambien. I put my ear plugs in, my eye cover over my face, and snuggle into my pillow for the next six hours. When I wake up, the plane is dark and quiet. I look over at Neal and everyone else; they are all asleep. *Rookies*, I think to myself. I reach up and hit the flight attendant call button. When she arrives, I ask if I can have my dinner now.

"Sure," she smiles and then heads to the galley.

I look down at my schedule. Right on time. I pull out my journal and start to write. My plan is to journal everything and create a book when I get home—maybe even publish it.

My dinner comes a short time later: chicken and rice. After that, I watch a film and chat a bit with Neal before going back to sleep.

I wake up just before it is time to land—again, right on time. It is six o'clock in the morning. I have just slept for a solid six hours. I am ready for the day and of course another flight, which is seven hours long. We are in

Taipei now. We find our next gate and settle in for a long layover of three hours. Viviane and I go searching for some food; all we can find is a deli.

When we get back to the gate, everyone is looking exhausted. I think everyone slept their normal eight hours when they got on the flight and now they've been wide awake for the past eight hours. Thank God I had Ambien. I sit down next to everyone and pull out my UNO cards. "Anyone up for a game?"

We play cards until it's time to leave. Again, I'm thinking to myself how grateful I am to have been prepared and to have brought the cards; otherwise, we would have been so bored.

**********

We land in Denpasar, Indonesia. I feel like we are in Mexico or Costa Rica; it's the same older feel, with that unclean look of the floors and walls. We meet up with Jared, our Indo-based leader. He is tall, handsome, and friendly. I can tell he is excited to see us. He gets us our Visas and we all line up to go through security. It's a long line and I am bored, so I pull out my phone to take a picture. There's a sign that reads: *Drugs are punishable by death*. I hold up my phone to take a picture when a man from behind the counter yells, "Ma'am! Ma'am! No photos!"

I quickly lower my phone into my pocket, a little scared. I look over at Viviane. "How was I supposed to know?"

She turns her head to the other wall and points to a sign: *No photos*.

I laugh. "Oh!"

We get through security, as Jared leads us outside to a table against the wall. At the end is a food stand resembling a hot dog stand but with nothing in the cart. We all sit down at the table and he says something in Balinese to the guy behind the cart.

"Are you guys hungry? Do you want any ice cream or shakes?" Jared asks us. Everyone orders something, but I decline. I am not about to eat a dairy product here—no way. I don't want to be sitting on a squatty potty the entire trip.

I realize that this could be my only time to buy a SIM card for the Blackberry, so I ask where the bathrooms are. Jared points in a couple different directions, saying that there might be cleaner ones in certain areas. There are small carts and shops with tents lined up along the wall and across the street. They all look promising, so I get up and start walking away.

"Wait," Viviane says. I turn back to look at her; everyone is staring at me. "I should go with you." She gets up from the table and walks over to me. *Damn.* I know she's just looking out for me, but now I might not be able to buy the card. I'll have to be sly. We walk across the street and along a cement sidewalk. The shops seem fairly new, with bright colors and clean walkways. People are sitting in little restaurant areas eating and laughing; it reminds me a lot of South America but with much more humidity. We walk to the end of the street without seeing a bathroom. Although we pass a couple vendors selling SIM cards, I don't feel comfortable enough to stop and buy one.

As we walk back towards everyone, Viviane sees a bathroom sign and we walk in. It's fairly clean but with an almost overwhelming stench. Interestingly, there are doors on the stalls. I would have expected a big room with holes in the floor. I walk past two stalls and push a door open. *Yikes!* There is a step up and then what looks like a toilet seat on the floor. I look at the walls; no toilet paper holder, which normally in the States you would see. These people don't wipe—and now all of a sudden I realize why I see shoe prints on a toilet back in the States. Those are probably from people who are used to standing on a toilet seat, not sitting! I quickly grab my roll of toilet paper in my back pack and prepare for the squat. Not bad . . . I finish up and rush out. Thinking this is my only opportunity to buy the SIM card, I turn the corner in the direction of the vendors. *Damn!* Viviane is already outside and waiting for me.

"What did you think of the bathrooms? It reminded me of Africa," she says, looking at me with wide eyes.

"Yeah, that was disgusting—but not as bad as I thought it would be. But the smell was horrible!" I replied, looking for an escape. Seeing that she was going to be on me like a fly on a Bali toilet, I figured I'd just buy the card and hope she has no idea what I am doing; after all, she doesn't seem tech savvy.

We walk back towards the group when on my left there is a vendor. I stop and look at the sign, which says in large letters: SIM. Viviane keeps walking, thank God. I pull out my blackberry and hand it to the man, who asks in broken English, "How many minutes?" I buy the highest priced card, hoping it'll do the trick. I pay the man and he inserts the card for me. Viviane is standing about ten feet away waiting for me, looking at another vendor's merchandise.

"Hey, there," I say as I approach. We are not too far away from the group, so I'm hoping they didn't see what I bought.

"Already buying souvenirs?" She asks, looking up and smiling at me.

Secretly I push the blackberry deeper into my pocket. "Yeah, things are so cheap here!"

We walk back to the group and sit down. The shakes everyone ordered are sitting on the table and everyone is having a good time, laughing and chatting. I feel much more comfortable knowing I am connected once again to the States.

**********

Several hours later we are boarding our flight to Lombok, an island southwest of Bali—only a short thirty-minute trip. It is close to seven o'clock, and everyone is looking wiped out. It is a very small plane, seating about twenty people; it reminds me of the planes I take to get back home from Portland to central Oregon. Everyone files on board; I choose to sit next to Jared. I want to pick his brain a bit about this trip and the work he is doing. I've always been interested in missions work, but much more interested in traveling abroad.

The plane takes off. It's a little rough getting into the air, with some swaying and rocking, but we get up and the plane gets steady. I look across and down the aisle at my team; everyone is asleep. *Rookies*, I think again to myself. It's way too early to be sleeping now. I turn towards Jared and tell him I'm going to take pictures of the team for blackmail later. He laughs. Slowly I take a picture of each person, bent over with tongues out, drooling, heads cocked to the side—some funny pictures. I almost fall onto Doug with laughter. I sit back down and start up a conversation with Jared. He tells me how he and his wife Jamie were called into the field and talks about their journey there. It made me think about my brother and his family, how they are in training to be missionaries—sounds like quite the field of work, even fun.

In a short time, our flight touches down on the tarmac. I look out the window at a small building, which must be the airport, and see a guy waving us in with lighted cones. The plane pulls up closer to the building and stops. Again, I am reminded that we are in a very remote location and will need to walk on the tarmac to get out of the airport. Once we get off the airplane, I pull out my camera and take another picture to memorialize my journey here. I want to document every moment of this experience. Everyone walks past me as I take the pictures, and we are soon inside. After getting our luggage, we all hop into a van to our hotel. Doug and Jared had told us we would be staying in a lower-end hotel tonight to get us adjusted to the rest of the trip. When we pull up to the hotel, I see a beautiful flower bush and a lit pathway. Everything else is extremely dark and from the looks of it, there's no power. We each grab our own bags and start following Jared, as he seems to know where he's going. He walks up to a little man and hands him a piece of paper. The man bows towards him and then hands him a bunch of keys.

Jared holds them out. "Do you all know who you're sharing a room with?"

I turn and look at Viviane. "I guess we're bunking together," I say with a smile.

"This way," Jared says. "I'll show you where the rooms are. The lights won't be on much longer." We all follow him down a narrow hallway and then up several steps. The walls are a burnt orange and the floor is dark cement. We stop at the first room and Jared hands me the key. Opening the door, I see a closet on my left and then the bathroom. It looks like a basic hotel room with the beds just on the other side of the wall. The floor is cement, though, and the room is very warm.

"Breakfast is at seven a.m., girls, so be packed and ready to leave in the morning." Jared shuts the door.

I look up at Viviane. "I am dying to take a shower!" Setting my bags down in the corner of the room, I realize this could be a good time to call Cruz. He's probably in school, but I can leave him a message.

"Yeah—me, too. This will be our last shower in a week!" She opens her bag.

"You can go ahead and shower first. I'm going to relax for a little while." I sit down on my bed, which is firm and covered in a typical bed spread. Nothing seemed much different from the West. If this is preparing us for the next week, this won't be as bad as I thought. Viviane goes into the bathroom and closes the door. I immediately take my blackberry and iPhone out. The iPhone doesn't work, so I text Cruz with my blackberry. I tell him I am almost to our final destination and that I love him. I also text the same to my mom and to Rhonda. I know they would like to see a message from me. Minutes later, the door opens and Viviane walks out with her wet hair and a white towel wrapped around her body.

"That was great!" She smiles. "Your turn."
I grab my bag and walk into the bathroom. It is simple, with a toilet, shower, and sink—but at least the toilet is a normal toilet.

When I step out of the bathroom after showering, Viviane is at the window looking out.

She turns around. "Do you hear that?"

"No. What?" I walk towards the window and hear a faint sound.

"It's the call to prayer," she says, looking out the window again.

"Wow, that's crazy!" I try to look out the window, but it's too high for me, even when standing on tiptoe. I give up trying to look out the window and check my phone: no messages.

"I'm taking an Ambien and going to sleep." I pop a pill into my mouth. Pulling back the covers of my bed, I suddenly realize how tired I am.

**********

I wake up to pounding on our door. I jump out of bed and open it; nobody is there. Viviane is sitting up in her bed rubbing her eyes. I can see the sun coming through the sides of the curtain. I grab my blackberry: six-thirty a.m.

"We've got thirty minutes before we need to be downstairs for breakfast."

After getting ready and packing up, we head down the hallway towards the lobby. To our left is a courtyard with white statues of people and a small pool. It looks so peaceful; I wish I could sit down for a while and meditate. After walking past the courtyard, the hallway opens up to a large room with high wooden beams. There are two tables on the left covered with white linens and chafing dishes, and on the other side are several long wooden tables with benches. Everyone is loading their bags into a white van outside. Afterwards, we walk back into the room, which is now set up for breakfast.

"We can eat now, but let's say a prayer first." Doug leads us in prayer, and then we all dig into the chafing dishes full of eggs and rice. Funny—I had imagined pancakes, bacon, and sausage when I was staring at the dishes during the prayer. It's my first let down so far.

Everyone takes their time eating except me. The eggs and rice are bland, so I don't eat much. I excuse myself from the table and tell them I'm going to the bathroom, but instead walk to the courtyard. Sitting down in a chair next to the pool, I say a prayer. *God, thank You for bringing me here. Thank You for the opportunity to change lives and make a difference in this world.* Feeling the warmth of the sun, I sit there a while longer meditating in prayer.

I am startled by the sound of a man's voice. "Anne, are you ready to go?" I look behind me to see Doug standing next to a statue.

"Oh, hi. Yes—isn't this beautiful?"

"Yeah, but there is much more to see, Anne," he says, walking away.

I get up, look around at the peaceful scene and take a deep breath. *Okay, God—you're in charge.*

We all get into the van and start down the road. It's a dirt road with a lot of bumps, making it hard to take any pictures. I give up and enjoy the scenery. There are a lot of people riding mopeds and dirt bikes past us, almost erratically—very unsafe. I remember Costa Rica being very similar. After an hour drive, we pull into a dirt parking lot, and for the first time, I see the ocean—it's beautiful. We all get out and head to a small shack near the edge of the ocean. Jared says something in Balinese and pays the man.

"Anyone want to try Indonesian coffee?" Jared holds up a small cup with black liquid in it.

"Yes, I do!" I love trying coffee in different parts of the world; so far I've never been let down. Cuban coffee, Costa Rican coffee, Mexican coffee—I love them all.

"It's a little thick," Doug laughs. "Good luck!" Everyone is looking at me, waiting to see if I am going to try it.

I walk up to the man behind the counter and he hands me a cup. "Thank you." I'm not sure if he knows what I said. I look into the little black abyss. "Ok, here goes."

I bring it to my lips and take a sip. It's thick but tastes delicious, smooth and yet strong.

They all line up for coffee and start chatting about how they slept; some didn't sleep because they were in a different environment. *Rookies*, I think yet again to myself; they should have brought sleeping pills.

We wait for the ferry for what seems like hours, but in reality is probably only an hour or two. The ferry is large and modern. We all decide to sit inside, where there is air conditioning. I pull out my phones to see if I can send messages. There's a signal but I don't want to risk getting caught.

"Do you girls want to play UNO?" I pull the deck of cards out of my bag. Their faces light up, and they all scoot in closer. We play cards for a couple hours, talking about our lives and what brought us here. Most of the guys are asleep, getting accustomed to the time change. The girls tell me they are a little jet lagged but starting to adjust. I had explained to them my sleeping plan on the way over and how I was able to adjust as soon as I got on our first airplane.

The ferry ride is smooth and beautiful; we pass several islands with trees and bushes lining the shores. In a weird way it reminds me of the San Juan Islands in British Columbia, and brings back memories of fishing on my dad's boat in Canada. I wonder if my dad is looking down on me now, proud of where I am and where I'm about to go.

We pull into a small bay; there are no buildings—just a few cars parked at the edge of the cliff. Jared tells us we are home and to unload our things. Minutes later he pulls up in a beige Land Rover Defender, and alongside of him is a grey Nissan Pathfinder. A man steps out and introduces himself as Jared's assistant. He looks American but has an Australian accent. A lot of Australians come here to Indonesia for holiday and end up staying because it's such a beautiful country. The man seems kind and helpful. I get into the Pathfinder with Viviane. I've been in a Defender before and it can be quite uncomfortable unless you're sitting in the front.

We drive through some narrow paths on dirt roads with passing mopeds; several times it looks as if we are going to hit them. After a couple hours, we arrive at a small town. There are buildings that appear to be businesses or restaurants. It reminds me a little bit of the Mexican town San Felipe, but instead of people inside making tortillas, they're probably making rice. The Pathfinder pulls up and stops in front of a small white mortar building. The Defender pulls up alongside of us and Jared jumps out. "Anyone hungry?"

I am actually starving. I didn't eat much at breakfast and I didn't feel like eating any of the Clif Bars during our ferry ride. We step inside the small hut; the ceiling is low and there is a fan in the back of the room blowing warm air in our direction. Flies buzz everywhere, and an old woman stands at a counter near the front. There are three small tables covered in red plastic table cloths, one on the left side of the room and two on the right; each table seats four. I don't see a kitchen or any back rooms. This is going to be interesting.

"Who wants eggs, and who wants fish?" Jared asks us, standing in front of the woman behind the counter. *Hmm*, I think to myself—*which one is more dangerous to eat? Probably fish.* So I decide on the eggs and sit down next to the rest of the girls. Everyone else orders fish; I feel like the odd one out. I wish they could just kill a chicken around here; I'm getting tired of eggs.

The food comes and I am happy I ordered eggs, as the fish doesn't look very appetizing. We eat quietly, probably all thinking the same thing: Is this going to give me the runs? Knowing that the bathrooms are undesirable, my biggest fear being here is getting sick—not being kidnapped, killed, or persecuted. For me, having to spend hours on end curled up in a ball on a dirt floor next to a hole is by far my biggest fear. If I have to eat eggs and Clif Bars every day, I'll do it.

After lunch we drive to another small village where our host family would be. There we would unpack and start our mission. We pull up to a cute house—or I should say hut. There is a small porch with a wooden overhang and a side yard fenced with wooden poles and chickens inside. *Looks like I'll be having more eggs.* We start pulling our things from the vehicles and loading them in the front room of the house, which is starting to get smaller each time I step back in; the luggage and surf boards are taking up the entire room. A small, older woman steps out and says something in her language; Jared responds and gives her a hug.

"Everyone, this is Ebo Cahora." He pats her on the back, and she bows and then smiles warmly. She is missing most of her front teeth, but I can see kindness in her smile—she is a good person. Jared had told me on the flight from Bali to Lombok that she has been a Christian for almost a year now and that she's one of only two people in her village who are Christian. Everyone shakes her hand and she continues to smile. When I get to her, I give her a hug. I don't know why; I just feel like it. She tugs my arm and pulls me to a side room where the only thing separating it from the front room is a long purple sheet. She grabs Viviane's arm as well.

"Oh, this must be our room." Viviane smiles back at Ebo Cahora. "Girls, this is our room." She smiles and walks out of the room. The room is small, about eight feet by eight feet. We all drag our bags in and spread out our air mattresses, which take up the entire back wall, leaving just enough room at the end of our feet for our bags. We will have to step on our own things to move around the room. I end up getting stuck at the end, which I do not want. If there's anything that crawls around on the walls at night, I am the lucky one to get tasted first. *Oh well*, I think to myself, *at least I won't know it because I'll be asleep with my Ambien.*

Doug pokes his head around the curtain. "We're going to the beach in five minutes!"

I look at the girls. They all squeal with excitement. "Yes!" I say. I can't wait to go surfing. I hear the waves are good here and the best thing is that the water is warm. I change into my bathing suit with my long board shorts underneath and a rash guard which I realize I hadn't run by Doug for approval. It's black and sleeveless, looking more like a tank top. I grab my snorkel gear. This is going to be a blast.

# leap of faith

We all load up into the vehicles. There are no surfboards because this beach isn't a surf spot, but from what Jared says, there will be some great snorkeling. The drive down to the beach is a lot like Costa Rica, with bushes and trees lining the roads, and even signs of monkeys from time to time. We keep stopping to take pictures. It's funny, because it's almost impossible to take a picture of a monkey; they are small, unlike the ones in our American zoos, and they blend into the trees—not to mention they are fast. By the time you get your camera out and locate the monkey in your view finder, they're off to another tree branch.

We pull up to the beach. It looks more like a bay, with cliffs surrounding the ocean. There aren't any waves, but nobody seems to mind—the scenery is magnificent, with blue skies, crystal clear water, and sandy beaches. We all jump out and grab our bags.

"Before we play, we're going to begin with a parable," Jared says, sitting down at the edge of the beach overlooking the ocean. We all sit down; the sand is warm and soft. Jared starts off with a prayer and tells us a Bible story. It's hard to focus, as the ocean behind me is calling my name out. We end in prayer and everyone jumps up.

"Anyone want to start by jumping into the ocean? It's a little bit of a hike but totally worth it." Jared points out across the bay to a cliff. I grab my camera and start taking pictures. I can't wait to show everyone back home how beautiful it is.

After shoving the camera back into my bag to protect it from sand, I look around and see that everyone is already walking towards the shoreline. I grab my snorkel gear and run. "Hey! Wait up for me!"

I see them turn into the jungle, and my jog turns into a sprint. The branches are hanging low. I try to push back the spiny bushes so as not to scratch up my legs. The path is small, just wide enough to put one foot in front of the other. There is a ledge along the left that drops down into the ocean. The path is climbing in elevation as I hike, and from the looks of it, it's probably about twenty feet. As I catch up to Viviane, the path opens up to a beautiful view of the ocean: blue skies as far as I can see, and the ocean is crystal clear. Viviane is standing just in front of me. Before us stands a rock wall with an old blue rope dangling from above. It looks like it had been nailed into the rocks years ago.

"Oh, hi, Anne. They're up there." She points to the top of the rock wall. I can hear their voices in the distance. I look down the other way over the pile of rocks I'm standing on. The ocean doesn't look too far from here — about ten or fifteen feet—but I'm not about to find out whether there are rocks at the bottom of that jump. It seems as if the team knows where they are going. "This looks far. We should just jump here?"

Viviane laughs. "Let's keep going. It won't be hard." She grabs the rope and starts climbing. I follow right behind. When we get to the top, Jared's sitting on a big rock looking at us.

"Go ahead; it's easy." He points across the cliff. I carefully walk towards the edge and look down. It seems a long way to the water. My heart starts to race and my legs feel weak. I can't believe it; for once in my life, I'm scared. *Come on, Anne, buck up—it's just a jump.* I look over at Neal, who's standing next to Jared waiting for us.

"Neal, will you jump with my snorkel gear?" I ask him, holding out my bag. "I'll get it from you once I get down."

"Umm—sure, ok." He grabs it and, with that, he jumps off the ledge. I look down, trying to see where he landed, but all I can see is rocks and grass. I turn to Jared. "Do we have to jump out a little bit? I can't see the bottom from here."

"Yes, a little bit, but it is straight down." He stands up. "Go ahead — there's nothing to be afraid of."

I look at Viviane. "If you go, I'll go."

She looks down and then walks a little bit further and takes a couple steps down to a lower point. "Let's just jump here; I'm afraid of heights."

I step down to her level; it's maybe a five-foot difference. "If we jump, we might as well jump up there." I point back up at the top where Jared is.

"Ok, but you promise: if I jump, you'll jump after." She steps back up to the higher point.

"Yes, I would never say that and not do it." I follow her back up. The nervous feeling in my stomach is getting worse, but the thought of climbing back down the way we came up seems just as scary. I'd rather take my chances jumping. I walk back over to Viviane. "Let's do it!"

She jumps out and screams on her way down. I hear a splash and then a bunch of screaming and hollering—she survived. Now it's my turn. Why did I tell her I would go?

"Come on, Anne—your turn," Jared says, standing near me.

"It just looks so far. How do I jump? Like a pencil?"

"Yes. Just don't put your arms out—you'll break your collar bone!" he laughs.

I'm standing there, now terrified. I've never been this scared in my life, ever. I just have a bad feeling. My stomach is heavy and turning.

Just then, Neal comes back up. "Hey, you haven't jumped yet?" He's all wet and obviously coming back for more fun. Maybe it's not that bad. I shake my head. "No. I'm scared."

"It's ok. It seems far, but it's not—you'll be okay."

"Ok, I guess I'll jump." I walk out to the edge of the cliff. My heart feels like it's going to jump right through my chest. I'm thinking that this is a far jump, which means it'll be a deep descent into the water. Knowing that, I'd better be careful with my air and ascend using as little air as possible, just in case it takes a while to get to the top of the water. "I just jump out and stay straight, right?" I look back one last time at Jared and Neal.

"Yep," they reply in unison.

I look down again, breathe in, and take the leap. I push off the rock and lunge my body forward, keeping my legs and body straight. The wind is rushing past me; it's a quiet whistling sound, and reminds me of the summit at Mt. Bachelor, but it's not cold. I look down and see the water coming at me. All of a sudden the water is all around me, but before I can start swimming to the top, I feel a vice around my body. It's as if there's a crushing of my ribs and sides. The air in my lungs slams out, all in one jolt. So much for using my air slowly. I look towards the top in panic; the sun is shining through the water bubbles; it's mesmerizing. I try to pull through the water with my arms but something is holding me back from extending them, so I keep my elbows close to my chest and pull through the water with my hands, as if to doggy paddle. I start pushing the water down with my feet, as if it's dirt or something of solid substance. Miraculously I reach the top and open my mouth for a breath, but instead there's pain. I can't breathe. I start to sink back down under the water. *No—I can't!* I say to myself... I push my body back up, this time swallowing some water and air. "Help!" I try to shout using the air I just inhaled. I start to sink back down. I'm tired and in great pain. *Why don't they help me?* I'm trying to open my eyes to see where everyone is, but I can't see. I hear yelling and screaming. *Why don't they see me?* I push myself up out of the water again. *The pain . . .*

"HELP!" I yell. Under the water again I go. Just then I feel hands under my right armpit pulling me up, and then under my left armpit. It's Neal and Viviane. "What's wrong?" Viviane asks.

I try to say something, but the pain increases every time I inhale. "I—" *Pain.* "Can't—" *More pain.* "I can't breathe," I say quickly.

"We need help over here!" she yells, and I see someone swimming very fast toward us. A head pops up out of the water. It's Angela. "Ok, you'll be ok—calm down." She swims behind me and grabs my head, pulling me back so that I'm floating on my back. The sun is in my eyes. I'm still trying to breathe, the pain increasing with every breath. I just want to breathe; my back keeps arching with every attempt. "Relax," Angela says.

I don't think she knows I can't breathe. "I . . . can't . . . breathe," I say, choking on air and water. "Can you feel your legs?" she asks, swimming me backwards towards the beach. "Yes. I . . . can't . . . breathe," is all I can say nodding my head.

"Stay calm, Anne. You'll be ok."

I see everyone swimming alongside of us. I'm scared. The pain is unbearable. "Anne, we are getting to the beach. Can you walk?" Angela holds my head up out of the water more so than before. "I . . . don't . . . know," I respond through the pain. Everyone swims up next to us and helps me onto the shore. I'm hunched over with pain but I am walking. I just want to lie down. We get up over the small waves crashing on shore and I lie down on my back. I still struggle for air. Doug comes up.

"What happened, Anne?"

I shake my head, signaling that I don't know. All I know is that I can't breathe, and I can't seem to find the words through my breath. "I . . ." I gulp some air ". . . can't breathe."

He bends down. "Ok, calm down. You'll catch your breath. Relax."

I try to look up at him, but the sun is blinding me. I close my eyes and try to relax. *God, please help me breathe.* I take a breath in through my nose and out through my nose. It's small, but I'll take it.

Viviane leans over and pushes my knees up to my chest and someone puts my arms above my head. It's not helping, so I push my legs back down. They're trying to help but nothing is working. I lie there for what seems like hours and finally start to breathe somewhat normally, with pain in my rib cage. I hope I didn't break any ribs . . .

"Hey, guys," I say, slowly standing up. "I probably cracked some ribs. There's nothing we can do about it. I'll just take some Vicodin when we get back." We head back to Ebo Sahora's house, and everyone is really quiet—a strange quiet.

We walk inside and everyone goes their own ways. I go straight to my bag. I grab my medication pack and start rustling through it looking for my Vicodin. I pop a couple in my mouth. *This should do it.* I get up and sit back down; the Vicodin hasn't kicked in yet. I crawl over to my makeshift bed in the corner of the room and lie down with my back on the air mattress. I don't know how much time has passed, but I'm startled by Angela when she enters the room.

"Are you okay?" she asks.

"Yeah, I think I cracked some ribs. I just took some Vicodin. I should be fine soon."

"Ok, good—dinner is ready," she says and walks out. The last thing I want to do right now is eat, but I make my way out to the next room where everyone is sitting in a circle on the floor. There is rice in two separate wooden bowls and what looks like noodles and chicken in another. Everyone is chatting about their day and grabbing food from the bowls with their fingers. Normally I would be grossed out, but for some reason I don't care. I use my fingers to scoop out some food and put it on my plate. I look down at it; it looks good, but I don't feel like eating it. I get up and excuse myself from the group. I walk into the bedroom and grab my blackberry. It's been at least thirty minutes since I took the Vicodin and I'm still in pain; maybe I should take some Advil, too.

I quietly walk behind everyone to the outside area of the hut and start to dial my twin sister. Sarah would know what to do in this situation. Although she's not a doctor, she always seems to know everything when it comes to medical scenarios—and if she doesn't know, she'll find out. It rings with no answer. *Darn it; she never answers.* This pain is crazy; I'm going to keep calling until she answers. I dial again.

"Hi, Anne!" Sarah answers cheerfully on the other end.

"Hi. Ummm . . ." I start talking before she can continue. "I hurt myself today jumping into the water; it feels like I cracked some ribs. I took some Vicodin, but it's not helping; do you think it would be okay for me to take some Advil, too?" I wait for her response.

"Well, I think so—it depends what exactly it is, because some already have anti-inflammatories in them," she continues. "Anne, what happened?"

"I jumped off a cliff into the ocean. I didn't hit anything. I'm fairly sure because I felt nothing on my feet," I respond, starting to cry. I am in a lot of pain and the reality is hitting me that I probably won't be able to surf and now my trip seems ruined. "I don't even remember going into the water, I just remember feeling like I was being crushed from all directions."

"Where is the pain?" she asks.

"It feels like it's in my ribs and on the sides, under my arm pits. Why?" It sounds like she might be on her computer. "What do you think? Did I break a rib?"

"Tell me where the pain is again?"

"Well, it's kind of hard to tell but I feel it in the front—like it's across my rib cage." I'm rubbing the area. "But my back hurts, too. I think the pain is radiating towards my back." I'm sitting outside, shoeing the bugs and mosquitos away. It's a very warm night and quiet—reminds me of the Costa Rican jungle. Just across the dirt road is a small hut painted a dull orange. I can see candle light through the open windows.

"Anne . . ." There's a pause. "Anne, I think you broke your back."

"What?"

"Yeah, it looks like you might have broken your back. But it doesn't make sense, Anne—you shouldn't be walking."

"I didn't break my back," I respond, now rubbing my back and standing up because I can't seem to get comfortable.

"It says here that you need to be careful because there could be internal bleeding." Her voice is getting serious now. "Anne, does your stomach look bloated?"

"Umm, well . . . I've been eating like crap." I look down at my stomach. It looks bloated but I ate a lot of glutens on the flight over and I haven't used the bathroom yet because the toilets in the ground scare me.

"I'm worried, Anne. If you broke your back—" She pauses as if to hide something. "Please just let me know in the morning if it's still hurting. I know it'll be late here, but call me anyway. Are there any hospitals around there?"

"No, I think the closest doctor is in Lombok. I promise if it gets worse I'll call you."

"I love you, Anne."

"I love you, too." I look up at the sky; it seems so peaceful here—why did I have to get hurt? The tears start to run down my cheeks. I probably won't be able to surf now; if I broke a rib, it'll take six weeks to heal. I'll already be back home by that time. I am miserable.

Everyone is finishing up dinner and starting to walk back outside to the porch where I am. I feel a strange sense of quietness, as if they had been talking about me. They probably think I'm one of those high maintenance women who constantly complains. They have no idea who I am. I'm starting to think we should have all gotten to know each other much more. A BBQ and a couple meetings didn't quite do it. I'd like to say something to them, but I feel as if I'd be misunderstood—so I keep my head down and stay quiet.

"How are you feeling, Anne?" one of my teammates asks, sitting down next to me.

"I took some Vicodin, but it's not really helping much. I think I broke a rib or something." Just in that moment a wave of nausea comes over my body. I jump up quickly and start running for the bathrooms. I'm almost there when it comes up—it's all water. I spit it into the gutter trying not to hit the chickens, but they don't seem to mind. I walk slowly back to the porch where everyone is sitting. It's quiet again. I wonder if they heard me. I don't care at this point. I wander back into the girl's bedroom and lie down on my mattress. I need sleep.

**********

I wake up the next morning to the call of prayer. I didn't sleep well at all. I couldn't get comfortable, and the thought of being "broken" during the rest of the trip terrifies me. This is not how I thought I'd spend my hours in Indonesia—not what I had expected God wanted from me.

Everyone goes into the great room to eat breakfast, but I decide to stay on my mattress and nibble on a Clif Bar. I don't feel like eating at all, but I need something in my stomach for the Vicodin. I hear everyone talking about the day ahead of them, about all the beaches and surf spots and cool hikes. I'm sitting alone looking at the wall, wondering if I'll be able to do any of it. Just then Viviane pushes back the red curtain that separates the entrance to the bedroom from the great room.

"Do you want to come eat?" She kneels down over me.

"Nah, I don't feel hungry."

"You have to eat something, Anne."

"It's okay." I hold up my half-eaten Clif Bar.

"Ok," she says and walks back out. I hear them whispering, but at this point, I don't care anymore.

70

After a few moments, Doug walks in. "Anne, can I talk with you?"

I sit up. "Of course." Viviane walks in as well and kneels down next to him. They are both sitting in front of me with a look as if I were in trouble.

"Anne," Viviane starts, "When I was in Africa on my first trip, it was very hard for me to see all the children and the poverty in the streets, but after a while, I got used to it. These people don't know any difference."

I stare at them. I cannot believe they think I'm in shock because of the poverty and the culture here! All this time, they think it has nothing to do with the fact that I've jumped off a cliff and had to be swum to shore. This is ridiculous.

Doug then goes on to say, "We are here for you, if you want to talk about it."

I sit up a bit straighter as if to make my point. "Seriously? You think I am withdrawing because of the poverty?" I'm shaking my head profusely, "No . . . No . . . I am not going to downplay the poverty here, but I have seen much worse. I've traveled and seen some horrible things." They're looking at me like they don't believe me, even though they're nodding in agreement. "I am in a lot of pain; I deal with it in a different way. For me, I need to be alone and power through it."

"Ok," Doug says, getting up. "Just so you know, there aren't any doctors on the island. We'd have to take you to Lombok to get checked out."

"Yeah, I know," I respond.

"What do you want to do about today? Do you feel up to coming out to the beach with us? Jamie, Jared's wife, can come out and stay with you here at the house if you want," he says from the doorway.

"Ummm, I don't know—what do you think I should do?"

"It's a different beach; we'll be walking a little ways to get to the spot— if you're up for a little hike?"

"Can I bring my air mattress?" I ask.

"Sure. Actually, I think Jared has an extra one we can bring."

"Ok, I'll just lie on the beach and get some sun."

"Sounds good." He starts to walk out. "We're leaving in ten minutes." I get up and throw a couple things into my back pack, making sure to have enough Vicodin and snacks for the day. Everyone is waiting for me in the Defender. I throw my bag in the side door and look back to make sure Jared is bringing the air mattress. "Thanks!" I yell back at him as he straps it onto the top of the surfboards. We get in and head down the road.

The road is dusty; it reminds me of Mexico. Little men riding on mopeds pass us, and women in saris walk alongside the road with baskets on their heads. I wonder to myself how they tolerate this heat in all that. We start to get deeper into the jungle, and now, instead of seeing people, we see monkeys; and just like Costa Rica, it's hard to spot one because they blend in. The Defender stops for a minute.

"Look there!" Jared shouts, pointing towards the right side of the car. There's a small group of monkeys sitting on branches next to the road. Everyone pulls out their cameras and starts clicking away, but just then, the monkeys disappear. Just as we start to move on down the road, I feel a wave of nausea come over me . . . *Uh oh.* I scramble for an empty plastic bag in my back pack; I grab it and vomit just as we hit another bump in the road. The Defender stops and everyone is quiet.

"Sorry," I say stepping out of the side door. It feels as if it's the beginning of more. I take a couple extra steps away and vomit again. I feel better afterwards, and get back in, apologizing again.

Doug looks back from the front. "It's okay—it's probably the Vicodin." The Defender continues down the road. I am holding my bag of vomit, feeling like an idiot. I should have stayed back at Ebo Sahora's house.

A few minutes later we pull up to a beautiful scene. The drive was totally worth this, I think to myself, as I walk up to the sandy beach. There's tall grass alongside the sand, waving in the wind; it reminds me of Florida, but the view of the ocean is like nothing else. The beach resembles a huge cove with hills and cliffs alongside the edge of it covered in trees. I can see boats and surfers in the distance. Remembering the Indonesian surf video my friend Jack had shown me, I'm thinking the boats I see out there are for some serious surfers.

"There are some nice lefties out there," Jared shouts, pointing towards the waves. The guys start to run down to the beach, each one with a board. I look around and see that the girls are slow like me. *Good*. We walk down the beach about half a mile to a nice cove-like area. Doug is sitting on his towel with Neal watching the others paddle out. I set up my air mattress and sit down. My back is hurting from the hike, and I'm exhausted.

I look back at Doug. "I'm going to take a nap."

I lie back and shut my eyes. The warmth of the sun is beaming down on me. Although it feels good, I can't stop thinking about the pain. Tears fill my eyes; I can't believe this happened to me—and they all think I am a wimp. I wish there were some way to do that jump over again. As I lie there replaying the jump, I doze off to sleep.

"Anne, wake up." I sit up and look out at the ocean, then down at the water coming up towards the end of my mattress. "The tide is coming up." Viviane is pointing at the wet sand down at my feet.

"Crap!" I jump up and quickly grab my mattress and bag to slide it away from the water. I look up to see that there is higher ground, but it is full of broken branches and trees. It looks as if there was a storm that came through here and knocked everything down. I need to get to higher ground. If the ocean comes up this far, there is no way I can swim or even wade through it. I look over at Jared and Viviane and they are hanging their bags in the trees. I can't do that. I grab my bag and the air mattress and begin to run back up the beach towards the vehicles. I look down at my feet to see the ocean starting to hit my feet. I stop to breathe the pain away. *Okay, Anne, you can do this—you're half-way there.* I adjust my back pack, tuck the air mattress under my arm, and sprint up the beach, and then up the hill to where the vehicles are parked.

I get to the top and sit down on a stump. My breathing is heavy and the pain is intense. I unzip my back pack to pull out my bottle of Vicodin. I pop two in my mouth and wash it down with water. I have no idea where everyone is, but at least I know they will have to eventually make their way back here to leave.

After a couple hours, I start to hear voices from behind me. I turn around and look towards the vehicles: it's Doug, Viviane, Jared, and Neal.

"The tide came up so we had to hike through the trees and up the road."

"Where's everyone else?"

"They're right behind us."

"I'm glad I left when I did then," I say, standing up. "There's no way I could have done that hike." They are all sitting down around me in the sand.

"You missed it," Jared laughs. "Doug got caught in the current and couldn't paddle back in."

"Seriously?" I look at Doug; his face is turning red with embarrassment. "What happened?"

"I had to paddle back out and help him to shore," Jared laughs.

"Sorry, man, I'm out of shape." Doug laughs and pats his gut.

"Are you hungry? We brought food." Jared pulls out some brown bags in the shape of cones. He hands me one. It feels squishy, so I carefully un-wrap the top edge of it to see rice, noodles and tiny pieces of chicken. It smells wonderful. I look over at everyone else; they are using their fingers to pull the food out to eat it. I hadn't realized how hungry I am, so I take a small bite—*yummy*. The flavors and spices are incredible. I sit back and look down at my feet. The warm sand between my toes feels so good, but I suddenly feel nauseous. I jump up quickly and run into the bushes to vomit.

When I get back to the group, everyone is done eating. Nobody seems to know that I ran off to get sick. I sit down on my air mattress and look at my lunch, basically untouched. I don't feel hungry any longer, so I put it in the community trash bag. I lie back on the air mattress and close my eyes, exhausted.

*********

Several hours later I am awakened by laughter. I open my eyes to the bright sun, high in the sky. Sitting up, I grab my sun glasses and look out on the ocean; the tide is out and everyone is coming up the hill with their surf boards. Viviane is sitting next to me with a book in her hands.

"How do you feel, Anne? You were asleep for a long time."

"I actually feel really good." I sit up straighter and stretch my arms out. "I think I just needed some good rest. How long was I asleep?"

"I don't know. I've lost total track of time here. You might have been asleep for two or three hours."

Just then Doug comes up the side of the hill from the beach. "We're going to head back to Ebo Sahora's house."

On the ride back to the house, I vomit several times, most of it dry heaving. The pain comes back and twice as much. All I want to do is lie on my mattress and cry. We get back to the house with everyone going their separate ways; I go directly to bed. The pain is intense. I can't seem to get comfortable, so instead I sit up and try to meditate. Unable to concentrate, I give up and grab my phone, but just then the girls come into the room.

"Dinner time," Viviane says with a big smile, hanging her towel on a chair in the corner of the room. "Are you hungry?"

"No, I'm not. I'm in a lot of pain right now." Tears fill my eyes.

"Oh, I'm sorry, Anne. Can I do anything for you?"

"No, but thank you." I look down so she can't see the tears. She leaves the room and I continue to cry through the pain. I can hear everyone having a good time in the other room. I say a prayer hoping that God might miraculously take the pain away.

After dinner Doug comes to the door to tell me there is a witch doctor on the island that does massages and that I could try it out if I wanted to. I politely tell him no, and he suggests that Ebo Sahora wants to help me by giving me a massage. I agree as long as there is no witch craft involved.

When I walk into her bedroom, there is a full-sized bed up against the wall, covered in a pretty red quilt and candles lit on each side of the room. There is incense burning on one side of the room and an area set up with glass jars of oils. She has me lie down on her bed, chest down. She begins to rub oils onto my back while saying something. I close my eyes, praying that she is not chanting anything weird—I hope she's just praying to God. After an hour or so, I am feeling a little better, but I still go back to my mattress and lie down.

I must have fallen asleep because when I open my eyes again, all the lights are off. I am still dressed in my beach clothing, so I slowly crawl off my mattress, being careful not to wake Viviane, who's lying next to me. I use my flashlight to find my sweats and a shirt. The pain is still intense, so after changing I walk into the other room and sit against the wall. I look at my phone; it's daytime in the States right now—and then it hits me: I need to call Alexis and Ethan, my friends who live in Bali. They would know what to do.

It's late, and I'm not sure if they're awake, so I send a text message. *Hi, Alexis. This is Anne. I hurt myself a couple days ago jumping into the ocean. I think I may have broken some ribs.*

Seconds later my phone lights up with an unfamiliar number. "Hello?"

"Anne, it's me, Ethan."

"Hi, Ethan!" I feel relieved to hear a familiar voice. Ethan is originally from Australia, so he has the voice of an angel. I have always admired the Australian accent, not to mention, I find it sexy, too.

"Anne, what the bloody hell did you do?"

"Well, a couple days ago when we first got here, I jumped off a cliff into the ocean. I didn't hit anything." I take a deep breath. "At least, I'm pretty sure I didn't."

"Are you in pain?"

"Yes. It hurts a lot. I've been taking Vicodin, but it's not really doing anything."

"You need to stay put and stop moving around. You need to go to the hospital first thing in the morning," he says in a loud and stern voice. I can hear Alexis talking in the background.

"Yeah, but there aren't any hospitals here. I don't know what to do."

"Anne, we need to get you out of there."

Alexis gets on the phone. "Hi, Anne. I'm so sorry you got hurt. How far are you from Bali?"

"I think pretty far," I respond, with tears rolling down my face. The reality that I am so far away from home is starting to hit me. "We flew from Bali to Lombok, and then took a five-hour ferry to get here."

Ethan gets back on the phone. "You need a helicopter!"

"Really?" A helicopter seems so extreme.

"Anne, if you messed up your back, you don't want to take the chances and become paralyzed."

"Yeah, I guess so." Now this is becoming bigger than I had ever imagined. A helicopter—how is that going to happen?

"I am going to start calling around for you. You need to be ready in the morning to leave. Can you do that?"

"Yeah."

Alexis gets back on the phone. "Does your family know what's going on?"

"Yes, sort of. I called my sister yesterday."

"Ok. What's her number? I'll call them. You need to rest."

"Thank you." My breathing is heavy and the tears are uncontrollable. I am so blessed to have such great friends; I don't know what I would do without them. After the seeming indifference and misunderstanding of my teammates, it is a great consolation to have friends who exhibit genuine compassion and concern for me. I give them my sister's information before hanging up, deciding to touch base first thing in the morning. The plan is to get me into Bali tomorrow.

I hang up the phone and text Dave. I tell him what happened and that I will probably be airlifted off the island in the morning. I return to the room and crawl over to my mattress. The pain is intense and lying down isn't helping, so I sit on my knees and hunch over with my head on my pillow. As I think about that last couple days—the flight, the beaches, and the jump that changed everything—I start to cry again. I guess I am loud, because Viviane reaches over and starts rubbing my back very gently, as if to comfort me. We don't say anything . . .

# diagnosis

The next day everyone is up and moving about, getting ready for their day. Doug pops his head around the curtain. "Jamie is on her way here." Jamie is Jared's wife and she's close.

I sit up. "Umm, can I talk to you for a few?"

He comes into the room and kneels down at the foot of my mattress.

"I called my friends in Bali last night." He's sitting there really quiet, looking at me. "Well, they want me to see a doctor today."

"Ok," he responds, shifting his weight. "Well, Jamie is on her way and she can take you to Lombok. I talked to Jared and he says there aren't any machines here on the island that can help determine what's wrong with you."

"Ok, yeah. I didn't think there would be." I'm trying to figure out how to tell him that my friends want me to be airlifted.

"There is a clinic in Lombok that should have an X-Ray machine. If they determine you need to go to a hospital, then Bali won't be too far."

"How will I get to Lombok?"

"Jamie will take you on the ferry. She knows where to go—don't worry. You'll be safe."

"Ok." I still don't know how to tell him that the ferry isn't a good idea.

"She should be here in a couple hours. We're going on a hike today, but we'll wait until she gets here before we leave." He stands up and walks out.

I am such an idiot! Why didn't I tell him no, that I need a helicopter? I grab my phone and dial my sister's number.

"Anne?" she answers on the other end. "I talked to your friends, Alexis and Ethan." "They said they're going to airlift you out of there. Anne, you need to be very careful. You might have broken your back, and if you move the wrong way . . . you could be paralyzed."

"Okay. I'll be careful." I sit up against the wall, still on my mattress. Maybe I am naïve, but I am still thinking that the problem isn't my back.

Everyone is making such a big deal that I might have broken my back, but it doesn't seem to faze me.

"Ethan is working on getting the helicopter; he said he already had it this morning."

"Yeah, he's a very connected man," I say with a smile. It's good to know people like them.

"We're also working with the church. Mom has been emailing and talking to someone. Oh—and Bridget is sending out an update with all your prayer partners so that they know what's going on."

"Okay. Thank you, Sarah."

"Does Cruz know what's going on? Have you talked to him or Jeff?"

"No, I don't want Cruz knowing, so don't tell Jeff, either, or he'll tell Cruz."

"Don't worry. I won't say anything."

"Thanks. I'd better go; I need to figure out how to tell Doug that a helicopter is coming for me." The thought of arguing with him right now while I am in excruciating pain does not sound fun. We hang up the phone and I walk into the other room. Doug is standing in the corner of the room with Jared whispering something. They both stop talking and look up at me.

"Doug." Jared walks out of the room and Doug walks over to me.

"I talked to my sister and my friends in Bali. They want me to take a helicopter over to Bali." Okay. There! I got it out! He's standing there staring at me, as if he doesn't know how to respond.

"Ummm," he goes on stuttering, "Jamie is on her way and she'll take you to Lombok. There's no reason for a helicopter."

"Well . . ." I am nervous now, "If something is wrong with my back—" My phone rings. It's Ethan. "Sorry, I need to answer this."

Ethan asks, "Anne, does the church have insurance?"

I have no idea. I am thinking to myself how silly it is that I don't know this. Holding the phone down at my side, I look at Doug and ask if the church has insurance.

"Yes, I'll go get it." Doug walks out of the room.

"Yeah, they do," I respond into the phone.

"Ok, good. I need the information for the helicopter company." Ethan sounds very much under control and calm. "They can come get you, but they have to take off before one o'clock."

"Cool. They wanted me to take a ferry over to Lombok."

"Lombok? Bloody hell you're not!" he yells into the phone. "You don't mess with your back, Anne, it's not worth it." Then he continues on about how he knew someone that is paralyzed because he didn't take the right precautions.

Doug walks back into the room with a small piece of paper folded up. "Ok, I have it. I'll send you a picture of it."

We hang up and I send him a picture of the insurance card. Not too much longer, Jamie walks into the hut. She is a very pretty woman with long brown hair and stunning facial features, standing close to six feet tall, with beautiful green eyes.

"Hi. You must be Anne?" She shakes my hand with a smile. "Sorry we aren't meeting under better circumstances."

"Yeah—me, too." I sit down in the middle of the room on my knees; I can't seem to get comfortable.

"Are you ready to go?" She looks around the room. She must not be aware that a helicopter is coming for me.

"Umm, I think a helicopter is coming to get me." I shift from one knee to the other. "I have friends in Bali who think I should be airlifted. If I broke my back, I need to be careful."

"Oh, okay." She smiles, even though I see she is confused. "I am going to find Jared. I'll be right back." She steps out of the room.

I look at my phone. I'm surprised I haven't heard from anyone yet. I wonder what is going on. Doug walks into the room holding up his phone. "I am trying to get a hold of the church but my phone isn't connecting; I can't get any reception."

"Here," I say handing him my phone. "Use mine."

"No, that's ok. Jared has one. I'll see if his works." He walks out of the room again. Just then my phone rings. "Hello?" It's my sister.

"Anne, we can't get a hold of anyone at the church." Sarah sounds frantic on the other end of the phone. "Do you have any emergency contact numbers?"

"No. All I have is what I gave you guys." I am confused as to why they can't get a hold of my contacts back there in the States. "Try calling Bridget. She might know someone—and if not, she can drive down to the church."

"Ok. I'll call you back."

In a moment, my phone rings again. It's Ethan. He tells me the helicopter company can't come to get me until the church approves it. That must be why Sarah was asking about contacting people at the church. Ethan sounds frustrated and tells me the helicopter can't leave any later than one o'clock, but they'll push it to two o'clock for me—but we need to get the approval, because if it gets too late, then we have to wait another day. The helicopter can't fly at night. I start to panic because I am almost out of Vicodin—only four pills left. I have maybe eight hours.

I ask Doug to call the church and tell him that the helicopter company is waiting on the church to approve the flight. He tells me they should have already done it.

As I sit, waiting to see what is going to happen next, wondering if I should just take the ferry, I look down at the insurance information to see that the broker of record is a company I do a lot of business with. I quickly call my sister and tell her to call my contact at the insurance company; they might be able to get the ball rolling faster.

Ten minutes later, my insurance contact calls me to say they are waiting to hear from the church. All they need is someone to approve it. Frustrated that nobody is taking the reins at the church, I call my mom to see what the situation is. She tells me the church still hasn't called anyone back and that she had called the helicopter company to pay for the airlift directly, but they wouldn't accept her credit card over the phone.

I hang up and look at my watch: it is three o'clock. I take a deep breath and succumb to the fact that I would have to take the ferry. There is no way I can wait another day for the helicopter. Just then, my phone rings. It's Ethan.

"Anne, where are you? The helicopter is leaving right now and we need to know exactly where you are." I smile. It's actually going to happen; this is actually happening.

"I have no idea."

"Ok, hand the phone to Doug."

I look at Jamie. "Do you know where we are?"

She shakes her head. "Hold on." She walks out of the room.

Doug walks in. "Here—hand me the phone." He takes the phone outside.

I overhear them talking about getting the exact coordinates for the flight crew. Doug doesn't seem to know how to look it up on the phone, so Ethan has to explain it to him, but eventually they figure it out and Doug hands the phone back to me.

"They are on their way," Ethan says. "The helicopter should get there in an hour or so. There is an old air field a mile away where you'll meet them."

"Thank you, Ethan. Did the church finally call them?"

"No, they didn't, but don't worry about that," he says in his Australian accent.

"Thank you so much, Ethan." I have no idea how that worked out and how it is the helicopter company agreed to take off so late, but it worked out.

"Alexis will meet you at the hospital. I'll come by tonight. Anne, don't worry. Everything will be okay." His voice is reassuring; I feel better already knowing they have the situation under control. I put my phone away and look up. Doug and Jamie are standing in the doorway. "Jamie is going to go with you; she will be with you the whole time, okay?"

I look at Jamie and she smiles reassuringly. "Ok."

"You need to pack up what you can and we'll get the rest to you later."

I go into the room and put some clothes in my back pack and the rest of my things in my large bag that I shared with Viviane. I don't want her to have to pack up my stuff. I give my air mattress and my blanket to Ebo Cahora; I figure I won't need it the rest of the trip, and if I did another trip, I'd just buy another mattress.

Packing up is surreal, almost like a dream—as if I am watching everything happen.

My phone rings. It's an unknown number. "Hello?"

"Hi, Anne. This is Pastor Barlow."

"Hi." I can't believe the pastor is actually calling me. This is my favorite pastor of all time and he's calling me. I smile.

"I heard what happened and I just wanted you to know a helicopter is on its way. We'll get you to a hospital and find out what's going on, okay?" He seems concerned but in a hurry to get off the phone at the same time.

"Thank you, Pastor." I finish packing and sit down. I decide to take in my last moments on the porch. It's very warm and humid outside; the air seems still, as if everything has stopped around me. As I sit and look across the street at the chickens, I realize I am going to be airlifted—taken by helicopter to a hospital. This is something my family would discuss often, because while growing up, we lived in a very remote area; whenever there was a horrible accident, people would have to be airlifted. We bought a special membership every year to have that benefit—and now, it's my turn to be airlifted. *This is crazy.* I'm not excited, and I'm not scared. I can't seem to find any emotion.

"Helicopter is going to be here soon. Let's get you to the field," Doug says, walking onto the porch.

We put my bags in the Defender; Doug gets into the driver's side and Jamie in the front passenger seat. I open the back door and slide in. Looking around, I wonder how I should protect myself on this ride. I decide to sit sideways on the seat with my knees up towards my chest; the pain seems a little less when I get into a fetal position. The ride is slow and bumpy, but Doug does a good job driving. We don't go too far—only ten minutes or so. We pull into a lush field, overgrown with tall grass and bushes. There is one tall building with boarded-up windows; this must be the old air field.

We walk out onto the field. It's surrounded by lovely trees—a view I'd only see in a post card. I pull my camera out and take pictures; I hope I'll be able to take some on the ride, too. Just then the helicopter comes in and lands. It's a beautiful orange and white chopper. I've been in helicopters before, but this one is nice and big. A guy jumps out and runs over to us. He says something to Doug and then runs back over to the helicopter. Eventually the blades slow down, and another man jumps out with a stretcher and a bag.

They put the stretcher on the grass and tell me to lie down. It seems odd lying down on this thing on the field, only inches off the grass. Then the guy bends over me and all of a sudden air starts to fill the stretcher and I can't move. I am fully stabilized. On the count of two, the men lift me up off the ground and carry me to the helicopter. For the first time I'm scared. If they drop me, I'm definitely going to be paralyzed. Somehow they put me in the side of the helicopter; my feet are in the front next to the pilot and my head is in the back of the helicopter where the passengers sit. Jamie appears on the other side of the helicopter along with Doug. He hugs her and waves good-bye to me. I can't hear anything over the engine, but everything seems to be going smoothly. The guy that put me in the stretcher sits up next to me and starts to take my vitals as Jamie sits facing him. I look at her and she smiles, reassuring me that everything will be okay. Just as we are about to take off, the medic sitting next to me leans over and yells, "I'm going to give you morphine, okay?"

I smile at him and nod yes. As soon as he injects the morphine, I start to feel better. The helicopter lifts up off the field. Here we go.

**********

The flight is beautiful. I am able to lift my head up and look down to the scene below. It seems as if it is straight out of a movie; all of the islands we fly over are lush and green. The ocean sparkles. As we soar through the skies towards Bali, it starts to rain. I can't see much of anything except the rain moving across the windows, so I put my head back and close my eyes. I awake to the doctor shaking my shoulder. I look at him and he points to the ground. We are landing on a helicopter pad. It's still raining, and there are a bunch of people with cameras and umbrellas surrounding the landing area.

After we land, the helicopter is pulled into a hangar where the door to the helicopter opens. I can see the people trying to get into the hangar. Strange—I think they're trying to get to me. A few men lift my stretcher out of the helicopter and put me into an ambulance waiting nearby. I see Jamie following closely behind with our bags. She gets into the ambulance, the doors slam shut, and we take off. It's loud, with the rain hitting the ambulance and the sirens blaring. I can't hear what the doctors are saying, but every once in a while Jamie joins in on the conversation in their language. I have no idea what is going on, and all I can see are the two policemen behind our ambulance with their sirens blaring. Eventually we arrive at the hospital and the ambulance backs up to huge glass doors.

They pull my stretcher out into the hospital. There is another stretcher nearby that they lift onto. There are three Indonesian women standing by with a clipboard. As I get rolled into their emergency room, one of the women asks me to fill out some paperwork.

I look at the questionnaire and then at Jamie. "Do you mind filling this out for me? I think I'm too high right now to concentrate."

She smiles and takes the clipboard. "Of course I can, but you'll have to tell me the information." I pull my passport out of my bag next to me and hand it to her.

"I trust you with this. Please keep it safe."

Just then two men come into the room. "We need to take you for pictures," one of them says in broken English. They must have been told about me ahead of time because they all seem ready for me and know what they are doing.

"Yeah, that's ok." I smile. As they roll me out of the room, I wave good-bye to Jamie with an uncertain smile.

I lie back and stare at the sterile white ceiling and walls. This place is definitely brand new; I can almost smell the paint. They roll me into a big white room; there is a machine in the middle. On one side there are floor-to-ceiling glass windows. This looks high tech. A couple of the guys lift me up and lay me onto a narrow bed connected to the machine. The guy tells me I need to hold very still and to let him know if I need out. *Out?* I think to myself. *Where am I going?* I smile at him and say okay. The machine starts to move me backwards into a tunnel. "Wait!" I yell. My heart is racing. This is suddenly intense. The machine moves me back away from the tunnel and the guy comes to my side.

"You'll be okay. Just relax." He pats my hand.

I take a deep breath. "Ok. I'm ready." He leaves the room and I go back into the tunnel. The men talk over the headset. "It won't take too long. Just hold still."

A series of extremely loud knocking and clanking noises follows. After a while it stops, and the machine moves me back out of the tunnel. They come in and roll me into another room, and then another. Eventually I get rolled back to Jamie, who is on the phone.

She hangs up to tell me that the church knows where we are and that they will relay it to my family. As we sit and wait for the results, things seem awkward. One of us is going to look bad. Either she will on behalf of the church if the results come back with broken bones, or I will look like a high-maintenance person if nothing is wrong. We talk about our families back home and get to know each other a little better. It doesn't really seem to help, but it takes my mind off of the inevitable.

Just then two men and a woman walk into my room, one man holding a white envelope and the other holding a clipboard.

"Ma'am." He steps closer to my feet. "Can you lie back while I ask you some questions?"

"Sure." I lie back, holding my head up towards him.

"What happened to you? How did you do this?" He's stepping closer to my feet and pokes my feet. "Do you feel this?" He keeps poking.

"Yes. I jumped off a cliff into the ocean, but I don't think I hit anything."

"No? You didn't hit a rock?" He pokes my other foot. "Do you feel this?"

"Yes. I mean no—I didn't hit anything. And yes, I feel that."

He's looking at my responses to his poking as he's talking. "Ma'am, can you close your eyes and tell me where you feel it?"

"Sure." I close my eyes. He pokes my right foot. "Right foot . . . Left leg . . . Right leg . . . Right hand . . . Left hand." It's like he's trying to get me to trip up and say the wrong thing. Why doesn't he believe me?

I open my eyes and sit up. "I can walk." I swing my legs over to the other side of the bed and stand up. "I've been walking around for two days," I say with a big smile, and then get back up on the bed.

He's now standing next to the other guy. They're both looking at each other with raised eyebrows. He holds up the envelope. "Ma'am, you shouldn't be walking right now—you broke your back."

Those words hit me like a ton of bricks. I think I stop breathing for a second and the world seems to stand still. Everything is quiet, and all I can hear is my heart pounding. My face and my shoulders feel warm. I look at Jamie. I don't know what to say; I feel weak. I put my arms back to brace myself on the bed. "So, what does that mean?"

"Well, you are lucky you are walking right now. *This*—" he holds the envelope up, "this tells different."

"What now?" I'm trying not to be a smart-ass, but part of me doesn't believe this is happening, and the other part of me is scared. If I am not supposed to be walking, then how could I be? I don't like hearing from a doctor, a highly trained professional, that I am doing something impossible. How are they supposed to fix me if they can't explain it?

"Devi will get you checked in, but you will need to be admitted into the hospital." He points at the woman standing near him. She smiles and walks over to Jamie as if they have already talked about it.

He leaves the room and we finish up the paperwork. The nurse asks me what kind of room I want because they have different options. Some rooms are shared or private, and the private rooms have the option of a kitchen table. Jamie and I decide on the private room with no table, as we don't plan on having large numbers of visitors.

Just as I am being rolled up to my hospital room, my friend Alexis walks through the emergency room doors.

"Hi, doll!" She screeches across the ER with a huge smile. I sit up and reach out to give her a hug. Her embrace is warm and consoling; it is so nice seeing someone I know from the States, even though they don't live there anymore.

diagnosis

"How you are? Sorry Ethan couldn't make it, but he'll be by later or in the morning. What did the doctor say?" She is all smiles and very sweet, but talking fast. She is Latina, and has a beautiful accent.

"I broke my back." It's all I can say. I can't even find the words to say hello. I'm still in shock that my back is broken.

"Whaaaaaaat?! Oh, sweetie!" She grabs my hand. "Don't worry. You'll be taken care of."

As we ride the elevator up to the ninth floor, it is very quiet. Nobody says a word. They roll me into a large room with a couch in the corner and a flat-screen TV on the wall in the center of the room. The walls are white and sterile, and floor-to-ceiling windows cover one side of the room.

"At least you got a nice room," Alexis says as they walk in. She walks to the large windows, looks out, and turns around to smile. Her positive attitude is almost contagious, but I'm still in shock. Jamie walks over to the couch and sets the bags on it as the nurses set me up to the station connected to the wall.

"Would you like more pain medication?" The nurse asks me as she puts an IV line into my arm. Up until this point I haven't had any direct lines — only the one shot of morphine, which is starting to fade.

"Yes, please," I nod. I look over at Jamie and Alexis; they seem to be getting along well. The nurse leaves the room and another nurse comes in with a clear bag of saline to connect to my IV line.

Now that I am back to civilization, all I really want to do is take a shower, but I don't want to cause any problems, so I bite my tongue. The nurses continue to connect me to several different devices.

Over the next couple of hours I catch up with Alexis. We talk about everything they've been up to the last couple years since they moved from the States. She tells me about the boys and how they've been adjusting to Indonesia. Everything seems surreal, sitting here in a hospital bed, hooked up to a bunch of machines and talking to my friend. It wasn't supposed to happen this way; I was supposed to be having dinner with them and laughing about all the magical things that happened on the island.

**********

89

The following morning is chaotic, with nurses and doctors in and out of my room. From the sound of it, my case has been quite the stir among the medical community. A couple of doctors come in to test my senses again, poking and prodding me. Nobody seems to believe I am walking and moving about. At one point, I decide to take my Bible out and put it on my bedside tray. God must have some reason for allowing me to break my back here in Indonesia; maybe it's because I am supposed to witness to a nurse or doctor.

Most of the day is spent trying to get my pain under control. Ever since I found out my back is broken, my pain has been less tolerable; it must be a head thing. I'm not sure what they're giving me for the pain because of the language barrier, but it's not working. Jamie tries to help, but she's not that knowledgeable with medical terms in this language.

Just as I decide to take a nap, my cell phone rings.

"Hello?" I look down to see that it's my mom.

"Hi, Anne. How are you feeling?"

"I'm in a lot of pain; they're not giving me enough meds."

"I'm sorry, Anne. Have you gotten any rest?"

"Not really. Doctors keep coming in and out of my room. Mom, I guess I should have been paralyzed." The realization still hasn't hit me yet, but it seems pretty real.

"Wow, Anne. You have a lot of people over here praying for you." I can hear my mom crying. The sound of my voice must make it more real to her.

"Thank you, Mom. Yes, I'm very lucky."

"Sarah is here. Can you talk to her real quick?" I can hear the phone being moved with some shuffling noises.

"Anne?" I can hear my twin sister's voice on the other end. "Can you have the hospital send your records to me? I am going to have some doctors look at them here."

"Yeah, I'm sure they can. Let me check." I look up at Jamie; she's sitting on the couch reading something.

diagnosis

"Jamie, could you see if they'll email my sister my medical records? She has connections with doctors there in Oregon. It would be good to get a second opinion."

"Yes, of course." She gets up and walks out of the room. I tell my sister that I'm having it checked on right now.

"How do you feel?" she asks me.

"I'm in a lot of pain; whatever they're giving me isn't helping. Jamie thinks it's probably something low grade. They don't believe in narcotics and alcohol here like they do in the States."

"Ask them to give you morphine. They have to have some. Seems crazy that they wouldn't have morphine there."

Just then Jamie walks back into the room with a piece of paper and asks me to write down Sarah's email address on it. I tell my sister they'll be sending her the records shortly.

"Good. It's late here, but I will get it to some doctors first thing in the morning."

"Thanks, Sarah."

"No problem. We'll get the best doctors on your case, Anne. Hey, aren't you glad you didn't take that ferry?"

"Yeah . . . Sarah, I like talking to you right now, but I'm getting tired. Can I call you after my nap?" I'm lying back on my pillow and my eyes keep closing on me. All this has been exhausting, physically and emotionally.

"Yes, of course."

"I love you. Tell Mom I love her, too."

"I love you, too, Anne. Bye."

I quickly text Gavin, an old boyfriend. He would have connections to some good doctors. I don't wait for a response and put the phone on the bedside table. The pain is still fairly strong, but all I want to do is close my eyes.

**********

I wake up to a nurse taking my blood pressure. I look around the room and see Jamie sitting on the couch. The sun is still shining, so it must still be daytime.

"What time is it?"

"It's almost four o'clock." Jamie looks at her watch. "You've been asleep a few hours."

"Do you know if they emailed my sister the records?" I look at the nurse and she is connecting my IV line to a new bag.

"Yes, they did, and I talked to your sister already. She got it."

"Cool, thanks. What's this?" I look at the new bag of fluids.

"It's a narcotic. You shouldn't feel the pain anymore."

"Thank God!" I smile. This will be nice. The pain has been intense, even with my high pain tolerance.

"Yes, I guess they needed special clearance to give you a narcotic—as if your broken back wasn't enough." She laughs.

Just then Alexis and Ethan walk in holding something in a brown bag.

"Hello, Anne," Ethan says in his charming Australian accent. Ethan is a good-looking guy and a man's man; the women love him. It could be the accent or it could be that he has a wonderful personality, funny and charming.

I give him a big hug. "Ethan, thank you so much for paying for the helicopter. I will make sure you get paid back as soon as possible."

"I know," he says, laughing. "I know where you live!"

I give Alexis a big hug, too; she's always so pretty and full of smiles.

"How are you feeling dear?" She pulls magazines out of the bag and hand them to me. "Thought you might need these if you get bored."

"Thank you so much." I smile. "They finally got me on a narcotic, so now I'm feeling much better. Still some pain, but not too bad."

"Well, damn, girl—you walked around with a broken back for two days. You're a bloody trooper," Ethan says, sitting in a chair next to the bed. I look at Jamie, wondering what she thinks of Ethan and his forward attitude. She just smiles.

"Anne, I'm going to see what kind of food they have around here. It'll give you time to chat with your friends." Jamie walks out of the room.

After a couple hours, Alexis and Ethan head back home promising to return the following day with the boys. I pick up my phone and start texting my friends—first, Rhonda. She tells me she'll pray for me and to keep her posted. I don't have much information for anyone because I don't know what the plan is yet. I want to get second opinions before making any decisions. When I tell Dave, he seems nonchalant about my injury, telling me to get a lot of opinions and to rest. Just when I think I'm done texting my friends, I realize I should text my ex-boyfriend who was a professional football player. He might know of some good doctors. He responds right away with a phone call back to me. We talk for a while; I hear the true concern in his voice. He tells me he will get in touch with my sisters and help orchestrate a phone call with his old team's medical trainer; they are in my area and would know some great local doctors.

Jamie returns a little while later with some food, but I've already eaten. Every day I get to choose what kind of meal I want—funny, because I have to choose according to type: American or Asian. Although I love Asian food back in the States, for some reason here, all I want is American.

"I've noticed you don't eat the food they bring you, so I brought you a burger." She puts a bag on my bedside table.

"Thank you, but I already ate."

"Yeah, right. You mean you picked at your food?"

I laugh in agreement. "Yeah."

"You know what I'm craving?" I ask with a smile. "It's so weird, but I'm craving a grilled cheese sandwich and some tomato soup. But they don't have cheese here like they do in the States. I don't think I've had a grilled cheese in years."

"That sucks. I love grilled cheese sandwiches!"

We laugh and reminisce for a while about food in the States. I feel bad, because I'll get to taste it long before she does. It must be hard living so far from home and so far from civilization she is used to. I give her a lot of credit being out in the middle of nowhere, working for God.

*Ring . . . Ring . . . Ring.* I open my eyes to see that the room is dark, and grab my phone. It's my sister Sarah.

"Did I wake you?" she asks. I look over at the couch and see Jamie sitting up on her bed. I must have been asleep for a while because it's obviously night time. I look at the clock on the wall: two in the morning. It's around eleven in the morning there.

"Yeah, but it's ok." I look at Jamie and whisper that it's my sister, and she lies back down.

"You are going to need surgery. Anne, I've had two doctors look at your records and they both say you are extremely lucky that your spinal cord wasn't damaged." She continues, "Gavin called me and I hope you don't mind, but I sent him your records, too. He's supposed to get back to me today with a doctor's name. I've also done some research on spinal doctors in your area. Check your email because I sent you the list. There are a lot, but there's one that keeps coming up. Mom is calling a few of them today."

"I told Gavin to call you, so it's all good — and thank you for doing the research. I have no way of doing it here, since I don't have my computer."

"No problem. What are the doctors there saying?"

"I'm not sure. They just come in and look at me surprised that I'm walking, and then leave. I think they figured I'd go home to have surgery."

"Oh, okay. Is there a certain hospital you want to go to?"

"Yeah, Hoag. It's the best one around."

Hoag is where I had my son; a lot of money gets dumped into it from wealthy families in the Newport Coast area, so I would think there would be some great doctors working from it.

"Okay, I'll check into that. I don't think I saw any that work out of Hoag, but I'll check."

"Thank you, Sarah."

"I'll let you get back to sleep. When you get up in the morning, check your email and let me know what you think."

We hang up and I fall back to sleep thinking about making a decision on a doctor. It seems overwhelming; I wish I had a husband to make this decision. I nod off.

The next several days are spent researching doctors and receiving visits from my Bali friends. Each time they come to visit, they bring something: their boys, games, food, anything to entertain me. I am so blessed to have them as friends and of all places, here in Bali. One time they surprise me with sushi, and I almost cry. Sushi is my favorite food, and I had given up on the thought that I'd have any in a hospital in Bali, of all places.

By the fifth day, I have decided on a doctor back home: Dr. Jeffrey Donnald, out of a hospital in Orange, CA. I had thought I'd wanted to be at Hoag, but this doctor's name keeps coming up during our research, so I believe it is a sign. Even though I have decided on a doctor, the hospital here in Bali won't release me yet, saying I need to be cleared and fit to fly. It takes another day for the doctor in Bali to fill out the "fit to fly" form for the insurance company. The doctor wants me to fly in a medical air transport for the flight home, but I am able to talk him into releasing me on a commercial flight. He only agrees to it if I fly first class and with a medical escort.

After five nights in the hospital, my flight home is scheduled. At first, my flight is on a cheap airline, booked by the insurance company, but then Ethan steps in and changes my flight to a better airline with fewer stops. Up until that point, I hadn't realized that the insurance company will do everything possible to keep the costs down, but in fact we as the customer need to make sure we are taken care of and are comfortable. I again am grateful to have Ethan and Alexis there by my side, helping to make decisions. The medical escort has to fly in from Singapore, so our departure is delayed a day, but I'm okay with it, finally knowing that I will be making it back home; the thought of seeing my family again comforts me. My mom tells me she'll be there when I arrive to the States.

The morning the medical escort shows up to the hospital is surreal. I have spent seven days here in Bali surrounded by nurses, doctors, and friends, accepting all the difficulties—but now it is actually happening; I am going home. I called Cruz the night before to tell him I was coming home early and that I would call him when I landed. I had also told him that

Grandma was coming to town. I think he knew something was going on but he didn't ask; he just seemed happy to know I was coming home.

Alexis and Ethan come to the hospital to say good-bye. It is sad leaving them, and I promise to be back. They have done so much for me. I have no idea how I will repay them for everything. Saying goodbye to Jamie is hard, too. She has been by my side day and night, making sure I was getting the best medical attention and the right kind of drugs. I know that leaving her is taking the little bit of America she has missed back home with me. I also promise to be back to see her and Jared.

I am rolled with my bed to the emergency room, where I originally entered seven days earlier. Seeing everything again is surreal. The ER doors open and I'm taken to the waiting ambulance. There I meet my medical escort Lisa, a tall, beautiful Asian woman with short black hair. She is carrying a black bag, which I assume is her medical bag. They transfer me over to the ambulance bed and the doors shut. Lisa and I are whisked off. The last time I was in an ambulance it was raining, but today it's a beautiful day with the sun shining through the back window. Lisa and I chat a little bit, talking about Indonesia and what happened to me. She is from Singapore and has been doing medical transportations for many years, once even for a high-ranking Chinese gentleman.

Once we arrive to the Denpasar airport, they have me get off of the bed and into a wheelchair. For the first time in seven days, I get to sit in something other than my hospital bed. Lisa wheels me over to the Cathay Pacific ticket counter, where she shows them our passports. Lisa gives me a piece of candy from a bowl on the counter and I start eating. The lady behind the counter says something in another language while pointing at me, and then goes into a side room. Lisa looks at me and smiles. I smile and look away, pretending not to be concerned, but I'm wondering what is going on. Up until this point, things haven't really gone my way. Just then out of the corner of my eye, I see Lisa put the bowl of candy that was on the counter into her side bag. I look up at her in surprise and she winks. I laugh. The candy is good; I don't blame her for wanting all of it!

Just then the lady comes out and gestures for us to follow her. We go into the same side room and they start talking in another language. In between the discussion Lisa tells me that the airline might not let me fly because of my broken back. Several people come in and out of the room, asking her questions about me. At one point a man asks me if I am okay. I say yes, never better, and then a few minutes later we are released to fly. Even though we have the "fit to fly" form from the hospital, the airline has to confirm it with the insurance company and again with the hospital. I am so relieved they let us go; the thought of staying one more day is unbearable.

Lisa pushes me to the gate. By this time the flight is starting to board. She stops for a moment to look at our tickets when a man taps her on the shoulder. He says something in another language and she pulls the bowl she had taken off of the ticket counter out of her bag. He takes it from her, then pats her on the shoulder. They both laugh and he walks away. I pretend not to notice and fumble with my phone.

She wheels me onto the plane. I have never traveled in first class internationally before, but I've seen photos Dave had sent me when he traveled to China for business. It is spectacular, to say the least. Each seat is private with a TV, reclining chair, power outlet, closet, blankets, and phone. Lisa sits to the right of me in her private area, but if we stand up, we can see each other. She gets me all settled in and tells me to let her know if I need anything.

I fall asleep right away but wake up several hours later. The plane is dark, with only illuminated floor lighting. I get up and look over at Lisa. She is awake reading something. I want to see what the rest of the airplane is like, so I start to walk towards the front part of the plane. Just as I get to the bathroom area, I hear a voice over the intercom: "We apologize for the interruption, but if there are any medical professionals on board—a nurse or a doctor—can you please alert your flight attendant?" I rush back to my seat and look at Lisa. I try to tell her I am okay, but she can't hear from across our seats, so instead I give her a thumbs up. I don't want her to think something has just happened to me. She smiles, gives me a thumbs up, and walks towards the back of the plane. I sit down, wondering what is going on. Gosh—could this be why I broke my back in Indonesia—so she could be on this flight and save someone's life?

Sometime later, Lisa comes up to the side of my seat. She tells me that a man in the back was having heart problems and she has him all set up on oxygen; she says he'll be okay, but she'll be sitting back there with him for a while and that if I need anything to let the flight attendant know.

I sit there for hours, watching movies and sleeping on and off. It's funny, because I am not on any time schedule as I had been on the trip over. We arrive to Hong Kong, where Lisa and I have lunch in a nice area of the airport and then wait for our connecting flight in the Cathay Pacific first class lounge. Again, I've never seen anything like it—everything is so luxurious and spacious. The thought of ever flying coach international again is disappointing. I'm going to have to really plan out my return trip.

After a couple hours in the lounge, we get on our final flight home to the States. Again, it is luxurious, much like the first flight. We sit close to each other, but this time I am exhausted, so I don't think I'll be awake much to talk. Just as the flight takes off, I fall asleep.

# family love

I'm awakened by a flight attendant, who has something in her hand. "She told me to give this to you." She points in Sarah's direction. I look down at a small plastic cup; it's my pills. Sarah has been giving me my meds every eight hours. I must have been sleeping for a while, because it seems like I just took these.

"Thanks." I smile, and pop them in my mouth with a swig of water. Although I have four narcotic patches on me that should last seventy-two hours, I also have other meds to take: vitamins, anti-inflammatories, and some I'm not sure of—I just do what my doctor tells me.

Before I know it, we are landing at LAX. The pilot comes over the intercom and says that everyone needs to stay put until the flight attendant releases us. He says that someone is on board that needs to get off first because there is an ambulance waiting. Sarah and I look knowingly at each other.

A wheelchair awaits me as we exit the airplane. Sarah pushes me through a special area and then outside where an ambulance is waiting. They put me on the gurney. I thought my mom was going to be here, so I call her on my cell phone.

"Mom, I'm here."

"Ok, good. How was the flight?"

"Great! I love first class!"

She laughs. "Good . . . Anne, we are at the hospital. I had planned to be at the airport, but I thought it might be better if I was here when you arrived and had your room set up."

"It's okay. I'll see you when I get there. Mom?"

"Yes?"

"Thank you."

"No reason to thank me, Anne. This is all just the beginning. You can thank me when it's all over."

I laugh. "Ok, Mom. See you in an hour."

The ride to the hospital is rough, rougher than any of the ambulance rides in Bali. We arrive at the back entrance to the hospital. The doors open and my stretcher is pulled out; they push me through the ER doors and yell, "The Bali Girl is here!" Sarah follows at my side, being sure not to leave me unattended.

"Where's my mom?" I ask the man that comes up alongside me. He is wearing a long white coat, and looks to be a doctor.

"Hi. How was the flight?" he asks, disregarding my question.

"Good. Where's my mom?"

Just then, I see her and Carrie. I hadn't known Carrie would be here. My mom runs over to me; her eyes are red and tears roll down her face. She hugs me. "Anne, I am so glad to see you! You have no idea how worried you've had us!!"

Carrie follows closely behind, tears in her eyes as well. "Oh, honey—so good to see that you're okay." She gives me a warm hug and holds on. "Your mom has been so worried about you."

Everything seems surreal, like a dream. I can't seem to find any emotion. I know this is a huge moment, arriving back to the States and now at my mom's side, but I can't seem to feel anything. I am happy to see my mom and impressed to see my friend Carrie—what an angel to be here waiting for me at midnight, and on a weekday. Carrie is a CFO for a very large publicly traded company, so for her to take the time to be here means a lot to me. I wish I could cry right now. I feel like an ass just looking at them.

"Your mom has a room all set up for you," Carrie says with another hug. "I am going to take off, but I'll be back in the morning. Do you need anything? What about Cruz? What are you going to do with Cruz?" She is such an angel, thinking about Cruz during this crazy time.

"Oh yes, he knows I'm coming home early. Can you pick him up from school tomorrow for me?"

"Of course, sweetie. What time?"

"Whenever, I guess." I have no idea what the plan is. I'm just rolling with everything.

"I have to be in the office for a meeting in the morning but as soon as I am done, I'll pick him up and bring him here. Is that okay?"

"Yes, perfect. I'll call the school."

"Okay, good night. Try to get some sleep. Love you, hon." She gives me one last hug and walks down the hallway.

The next few hours are a blur. They take me to my room upstairs and ask me to get into a gown. For the first time since I broke my back, I've been asked to get into a gown. For some reason, they let me wear my sweats and t-shirts at the hospital in Bali. After I change, they take me in my hospital bed to the imaging area. They tell me I need more x-rays, scans, and MRIs. I argue with them for a little while, telling them that the hospital in Bali already did it and that they had high-tech, brand new equipment. I didn't realize they wanted to make sure nothing had happened to me on the way over from Asia. I was thinking they just wanted to rack up the insurance money.

While waiting for one of the imaging rooms, I see a lady standing in the hallway. She is dressed in regular clothes, probably waiting for someone. She asks me why I am there, so I tell her what happened and that I've just flown in from Indonesia. She is shocked and tells me it is quite a story. She says she will pray for my recovery. It's the first time I have told my story to a believer. It makes me realize how much God has protected me along the way. So much could have gone wrong and yet it didn't. She tells me I am really lucky to be alive, to be walking. Hearing it from someone else and from an American is life changing.

I'm taken back up to my room after what seems like hours. My mom is sitting on the couch next to the bed reading.

"How was it?" She asks, putting the book down.

"Tiring. I want to take a shower."

"Um, I'm not sure if you can." She looks at the nurse. "Can she take a shower?"

The nurse looks at me quizzically. "Let me check." She walks out of the room.

"Anne, you need to be very careful. The doctor says any wrong movement can leave you paralyzed." She stands up, walks over to my bed, and grabs my hand.

"A lot of people have been praying for you." Tears are rolling down her face. She looks tired and worn out. I've only seen her look like this once before, and that's when she picked me up from the airport just after finding out my dad had killed himself.

As I think about this past year, so much has happened. I can't believe how much God has put me through. Why doesn't He stop? Tears start to roll down my cheeks as I look out the window. *God, why can't life be easy for me?*

Last year, my dad, who had been married to my mom for forty-five years, took his own life. It happened suddenly, as most suicides do, and it of course shocked my entire family. The hardest moment was sitting down to tell my eight-year-old son that his grandfather was in heaven. He had never experienced losing someone close to him before, so it was extremely hard to console him while still processing everything myself. I did the best I could to explain to him why a person would take his own life. At such a young age my son had to process loss and abandonment at the same time. Previous to my dad, my best friend had committed suicide when she was nineteen years old. Over time I learned that I couldn't have done anything to save her or change the outcome of her life. So when it came time to process my dad's death, instead of being angry and asking all the "why's" I reflected on my life with my dad, all the fun things we did together and all the fatherly advice he gave me. There was nothing that could undo what he had already done, the good and the bad.

It's strange how God prepares you for the road ahead. Looking back, my best friend's death and her suicide had prepared me for my dad's death, which brought my family closer together. The way my sister had reacted when she learned I had hurt myself, the way my family had rallied together to bring me back home—much of this is a reflection of the effect of my father's death on all of us. We all became stronger in our faith and ultimately stronger as a family. Looking back on my past, it seems as if God keeps preparing me for something worse.

*God if by breaking my back is preparing me for something even harder to come, I want out.* My face is soaked with tears and my head is hot. *I love You and trust You, but please give me a break . . . Please.* I then feel a sense of calmness come over me and the tears stop. God is telling me to focus on Him and that everything will be okay.

I tell my mom I'm sorry and that I'll be more careful from now on. Just then the nurse returns. "You can take a shower, but you need to be careful."

The look on my mom's face is indescribable; she looks shocked and mad but somewhat happy for me.

"Thank you!" I smile at my mom. "I haven't taken a shower in more than a week!"

I grab my bag and walk into the bathroom. As I unrobe I look at my back for the first time. The hospital in Bali had mirrors, but I am just now noticing that my back is swollen. It looks like I have a hump back or that I have huge muscles there, the way a swimmer's back looks.

After my shower, I get into bed. I have no idea what time it is. My mom is asleep on the couch next to my bed, and I don't dare wake her. I grab my phone and start texting my friends to let them know I've made it back safely and that I'm in the hospital. I don't hear back from Rhonda, but Dave texts back right away. It is around four o'clock in the morning, but he works odd hours. He tells me he's praying for me and to keep him posted. After texting with him, I nod off.

I am awakened by a nurse checking my blood pressure. I look around the room and see my mom still asleep on the couch. Being careful not to wake her, I say nothing to the nurse and just smile. She smiles back and finishes up, writing down the results on a clipboard.

"The doctor will be in here shortly," she says and walks out of the room. My mom sits up and looks at me.

"Sorry, Mom—I was trying to be quiet. The nurse was just here checking on me."

"Is everything okay?"

"Yes. She said the doctor will be coming in here soon, though."

"Good." She gets up and walks into the bathroom.

Just then the doctor walks in with a tall and very handsome black man next to him. They're both wearing suits and are very good looking. I've always had a thing for a man in a suit.

"Hi, Anne. I'm Dr. Donnald, and this is my physician's assistant Peter." He pulls up a chair next to my bed. I sit up and try to pull my hair back from my face, thinking what a mess I am right now, while there are two attractive men sitting three feet away from me. Not good timing.

"Hi. It's nice to meet you." I shake their hands.

He tells me he's been talking to my mom and that he will take good care of me. I watch his lips moving but only comprehend a few words at a time, not really taking in all he's saying. Again, this seems surreal to me, as if I'm watching a movie. He smiles, shakes my hand again, and leaves the room.

My mom walks out of the bathroom. I had forgotten she was in there.

"Shoot! Dr. Donnald just left!"

"How long ago?"

"Two minutes, I think."

She runs out of the room. A short while later, she returns with a piece of paper.

"I was able to talk with him. I took some notes." She holds up the paper.

"Good, because I don't remember what he said."

"He's a very nice man. You are lucky you got him as your doctor. Did you know he gave me his cell phone number and his home phone number while you were in Indonesia?"

"No, really? That's crazy. I don't know of any doctors that do that!"

"Yeah, he said he wanted to make sure you would be all right. Anne, I think it's a God thing that you got him as your doctor."

"Yeah, probably. So what did he say? All I got from our conversation was that it should be a simple surgery, maybe three or four hours, but he wouldn't know until he opened me up."

"Yes, and that he has your surgery scheduled for three o'clock this afternoon."

"What time is it now?" I look at my phone. It's eight in the morning. "Carrie is getting Cruz, right?"

"Yes, but I need to call Jeff to tell him what's going on."

The next several hours I spend on the phone. I call a few clients and then my ex-husband. He asks me a series of questions, and then I tell him that my friend is picking Cruz up from school, but nothing is set in stone as to whether he'll stay with me or with him.

Just before noon, Cruz comes running into my room with a huge smile. "Mom!" he yells. Carrie follows not too far behind, dressed in a suit, looking very pretty and professional.

"He knows," she says with a disappointed look. "He asked as soon as he got into the car. It's like he knew."

"No worries. It's okay." I smile. It's actually better this way; I don't have to tell him myself. I wasn't sure of what I would say; she saved me the heartache.

"Mom, I knew something had happened to you—I just knew it!"

Cruz and I have always been very close, almost as close as my twin sister and I. It's strange how in tune he is to me and to things around him.

"Are you going to have surgery?"

"Yes, honey, in a couple hours—but I'll be okay." I smile. He smiles and hugs me.

"Can I get up in bed with you?"

"Sure!" He hops up and snuggles close to me, wrapping his little arm around my waist.

Soon after, Olivia arrives. I hadn't known she was coming down from Oregon. It's like a mini-family reunion—strange, because it's all centered on me. I'm not used to all this attention. Just as Olivia is getting settled in, the nurses come to take me to pre-op. They tell everyone they can come with me, so my mom, Olivia, Cruz, and Carrie follow behind.

We go down several flights of floors before the doors open up to a busy floor. There are doctors and nurses going in all different directions; it looks like organized chaos. They roll my bed into a small room with a curtain separating us from the noise.

"Wait here. We'll start prepping you soon."

Everyone sits down in folding chairs along one side of the wall. Just then, my ex-husband walks in.

"What's all the commotion about?" He laughs. "They're acting as if you broke your back!"

Cruz runs over to him and gives him a hug. "Dad! She DID break her back!"

Jeff laughs and everyone else follows with uneasy laughter. "Yeah, I know, bud—I was joking."

"Oh."

"How are you feeling? You look pretty good." Jeff sits down in one of the chairs.

It's strange he is here; I wonder if my mom invited him. I look at my mom; she must know what I'm thinking, because she raises her eyebrows as if to say no. I look at Carrie; she has the same look as my mom but smiles.

"I'm on a lot of pain killers; I don't feel a thing."

Just then the nurses come in to take me to surgery. "Ok, it's time."

My mom leans over and gives me a hug; tears are streaming down her face. "I love you, Anne. We'll be praying for you." She is trying to be strong, but I can see the soft side of her that is scared to death.

"Thanks, Mom. I'll be fine." I give her a hug and hold on. "I love you."

"Love you, too, Anne."

Carrie grabs my hand. "Everything will be okay, and I'll see you when you get out of surgery."

"Thanks for all your help, Carrie . . . I love you."

She has tears in her eyes, too; everyone does but me. Again, it is strange—I can't seem to find any emotion. I know this is a huge surgery, and yet I feel that everything will be okay in the end. Cruz walks over to me, leans over, and starts to cry.

"Mom, when will I see you again?"

family love

"I'm not sure—maybe in a few hours. I'll be okay, honey." I kiss his
head and hold onto him. "You know that I'll always be there for you. I'll
always be with you, always in your heart, forever and ever."

"I love you, Mom." He holds on to me even more tightly.

The nurses start to push my gurney out of the room but my mom stops
them. "Wait—let's pray." They all stand around me and pray, even the
nurses. As they pray, I feel God's grace and peace cover me, more than ever
before.

**********

Some time later, I open my eyes and look around. Everything seems
blurry, as if I'm looking through a haze. I can't feel anything. I can't feel my
fingers or toes; I try to lift my hand to my face but I can't. I don't even know
where it is. I feel nothing. Where am I? What is happening? I can see a door
to my left and in the corner a bookshelf or counter. As I run my eyes along
the wall, I see a padded bench. I close my eyes; this can't be real. Where am
I? I open my eyes again, trying to make sense of what is happening. Okay,
okay—what happened this past week? Oh, yes—I remember. I was working
a lot and getting ready for my trip to Indonesia—yes, that's what I was
doing. I was in Indonesia . . . But how did I get here? This must be a dream.
*God, please wake me up out of this strange dream.* I'm scared and confused. As I
look over the room again, everything still seems blurry; it just doesn't seem
right. I can't be dead, can I? Otherwise I'd be able to look down on
everything. I can't figure out how to look behind me; what's behind me? I
don't feel a thing. I'm really scared now; I can't seem to look behind me. I
am trying to move but I can't. Is this a joke? Are there a bunch of people
standing behind me ready to laugh? Again, I try to move—nothing. If I were
dead, I would think that I'd be able to see all around me. Okay, good; I must
be alive. *Thank God. But God, why can't I move? Why can't I hear anything?* No
response. *Why can't I hear You? Where are You, God? Please, God, help me. I
love You.*

**********

"How's the pain?" My sister, Olivia, asks as I open my eyes. She's sitting to my right on a bench, and the sun is shining through the corner of the drapes.

"Not too bad."

"Good. They just gave you more morphine. Anne, they said you were on massive amounts of drugs when you came over from Bali, enough for a man twice your size."

"Really?"

"Yes, so they've had problems getting your pain under control. They don't want to kill you."

"Yeah, but I have a high tolerance to pain killers."

"Well, the doctors in Bali could have killed you!"

"They didn't." I smile. "How long have I been out? How long ago was the surgery?"

"Three days."

"What?! Where's Cruz?"

"Anne, when you came out of surgery—" she pauses to take a deep breath, "Cruz freaked out. He was hysterical. I didn't want him to wait for you, but he insisted. I told Mom not to cry and to be strong for Cruz, but as soon as they rolled you into the room, she started bawling! And then Cruz—it was crazy. I tried to calm him down, but I couldn't. You were so out of it."

"Where was Jeff? Where was Carrie?"

"The surgery took nine hours, Anne; it was only supposed to be four at the most. That's why everyone was freaked out. Carrie went home after you went into surgery, and Jeff stayed around for a couple hours but left, too."

"Where's Cruz?"

"He's with Mom right now. They went to get some lunch."

"Where has he been sleeping? Here?"

"No, he went home with Mom the night after surgery, and I've been taking him home every night with me. Mom's been staying here with you, sleeping on this couch."

"How's he doing?"

"He's good. I'm really proud of him, Anne. He's stepped up, been a big boy."

"Where's my phone?"

She hands me my phone and I look at it. Nothing seems to register. I see my friends' names in the text screen and try to read the messages; there are a lot. I hand my phone back to Olivia. "Will you read these and respond for me? I can't right now."

"What do you want me to say?"

"Just tell them it's you responding and that I'm fine. I'll reach out to them when I can."

"Okay." She sits back down on the couch with my phone and talks to me as she's typing.

"Did Rhonda call or text? I gave her your number and asked to connect with you."

"No. I've only heard from Dave."

"Oh, okay. Is there a text from her on my phone?"

"Let me check . . . Nope."

"Weird. I think she's out of town this weekend. She's probably busy."

Just then Cruz and my mom walk into the room. Cruz smiles a big fake smile and comes to my side. "Hi, Mom—you're awake."

"Yep! How are you? Having fun with Grandma?"

"Yeah. She just bought me a new game."

My mom pushes a chair over to the side of the bed. "Here, Cruz. Sit next to your mom."

"Thanks, Grandma."

He sits down and grabs my hand. I am lying on my back with the bed adjusted in an almost sitting position.

"I love you, Mom."

"I love you, too, bud."

My mom sits down on the other side "When's the last time they turned you?"

"What do you mean?" I look at here quizzically.

"They are supposed to turn you so you don't get blood clots or bed sores."

I then realize that I have something on my legs. I shuffle them under the blankets.

"What's on my legs?"

"It's an inflatable sleeve connected to a machine; it circulates air which keeps your blood circulating—high-tech."

"Oh, cool." Every once in a while I can feel the air being pumped in and it gets tight around my calves.

Just then a nurse comes in. "Someone is awake." We smile at each other. "How's the pain?"

"It's ok."

She grabs a black cord wrapped to the side of my bed. "Press this if the pain gets too much; it releases morphine into your IV—but you can only press it once in a fifteen-minute period of time."

"Ok. Thanks."

"And this," she grabs the remote for the bed, "this adjusts your bed position. You can lie down flat or sit up. And this right here," she points to the top of the remote, "controls the TV."

"Cool. Everything is right here."

"Yes. Let me know if you need anything." She points at the remote. "You can page me by pressing this button."

"Thanks." I take the remote from her.

Another nurse walks into the room. "You ready to move her?"

"Yes," the one nurse says.

Cruz gets up, as if he knows what's going to happen and stands by the door. The nurses get on each side of me, holding onto a sheet that's under me. "At the count of three, we are going to turn you on your side. One, two, three." The sheet moves under me and I turn to my left side. They stuff pillows on the back of me to keep me from moving onto my back. "Does this feel ok?"

"Yeah," I say, looking at her over my right shoulder. This is a bit uncomfortable, but what else am I going to say?

The nurse walks over to my front side and tucks a pillow under my arm and in between my legs, probably to keep my spine straight. Now I am really comfortable; it's like I'm cuddling with a pillow. My eyes start to close. . . I'm getting sleepy.

**********

Over the next several days, I wake up to see Cruz sitting by my side, and if he isn't there, it's my mom or sister. My sister informs me who texted or called. I tell her I don't want any visitors except Rhonda or Carrie because I look like shit. I still haven't heard from Rhonda.

Although I asked for no visitors, my friend Chloe shows up with a beautiful orchid and stays to chat for a while. I have to admit; it is nice seeing a familiar face. It makes me realize that true friends don't care what you look like; they'll still show up when you're in need. There are several other friends who bring flowers or come to show their love, but Rhonda is still missing in action. I think about having my sister text her, but I feel that if she wants to see me, she'd reach out to me. I am starting to feel hurt by her absence.

Early one morning, Dr. Donnald comes into my hospital room with his physician assistant Peter. He sits down at the foot of my bed and asks how I'm feeling. He tells me the surgery went well and that he believes I will recover a hundred percent. He explains that he had to go in through my ribs, just under my arm pit on my right side; they had to cut through my ribs and insert a small tube, and then they pushed a titanium cage the size of a D battery filled with some of my bones and some cadaver bones through the tube. The cage will now act as my vertebrae, keeping my spine from collapsing. Then they had to open up my back and clean out most of my thoracic vertebra ten and replace it with four titanium screws, fusing my thoracic nine and eleven. He smiles the entire time he explains this to me, making it seem as if it is no big deal. He explains that I will probably be in the hospital another week and that he doesn't want me to leave until I can walk up several steps of stairs. He also tells me that somebody will be coming to measure me for a hard cast, which I'll be wearing for two to three months. I ask him how long before I'm a hundred percent again, and he tells me that it depends on each individual—it could be six months or it could be two years.

After he leaves, I feel emotionally drained. The thought of recovering for a couple years is scary. I can't wait to run again—heck, to walk again. I look out my window and start to cry. I haven't cried in a long time. It's almost as if the reality is starting to set in . . .

Twenty-one days after being admitted to the hospital, I am finally released. Although I'm still struggling with nausea, mostly from the pain meds, they allow me to go home. My mom pulls my car up to the hospital valet area and the nurse pushes my wheelchair close to the car. Being outside for the first time in a month is surreal. It's bright and warm outside; it smells like summer with the scent of flowers in the air. The nurse and my mom both help me get into the car. It's quite awkward, but I'm able to sit in the passenger seat and adjust it straight up and down, mostly at a ninety-degree angle.

I'm wearing my turtle shell brace. It consists of hard plastic and goes from my chin to my hips, with Velcro straps on each side. The Velcro helps the cast stay in place to protect my spine. The cast keeps me from bending and twisting my back. The doctor told me I won't be able to bend, lift, or twist for several months because he wants to make sure everything heals properly.

The car ride home is rough, and I vomit a couple times. It hurts, but thankfully, my sister Olivia is here to help me. As we enter the neighborhood, a wave of sadness comes over me. I'm not supposed to be returning home this way. I look out at the pool—many memories, but none will be made there this summer. The garage door opens and I see a wheelchair at the entrance to the house. I haven't been home for almost a month, and this is emotional. My mom pulls the car half-way into the garage and steps out. She comes around to my door and helps me get into the wheelchair, and then pushes me over to the entrance of the house.

"Are you sure you don't want me to push you to the front door?"

We had discussed what would be easiest, as the many flights of stairs might wreak havoc on my back. I had decided I would walk up the two flights, with their help. I was being stubborn and didn't want special attention.

"Yes," I respond, looking at her firmly. "Is London outside?"

I had asked that they put my dog outside just in case she tried to jump up on me. I've heard that dogs can sense when people are hurt, but I'm not about to test it out with a broken back.

"Yes, she's outside." Olivia opens the door to the house. "Come on."

They both lift me out of the chair holding onto each of my arms. I walk slowly into the house. My biggest concern right now is trying not to vomit. I shuffle my feet to the first of twelve steps. Olivia holds my right arm as I climb each step at a time while I grab onto the railing with my left hand. We reach the top and my mom carries the wheelchair up. I sit down. That was exhausting, but I'm not going to let them know.

"Good job," Olivia says excitedly. "How do you feel? Any pain?"

"I'm okay."

My wheelchair is facing the pool table and I can see London through the sliding glass doors. She's got her nose pressed up against the glass.

"Can you push me over to the window?" I point at the sliding glass doors.

My sister pushes me closer to the glass and the emotion overwhelms me. My face feels hot and tears come uncontrollably. I'm stuck in a wheelchair and everything is out of my control. London starts whining loudly and jumping against the window; I've never seen her like this before.

"She must know that you're hurt; she wants to comfort you." Olivia kneels down next to me. "My dog Jack does that when something is wrong with me or Luke."

I can't respond to her because I am choking back tears. I look away so she can't see me. I feel so stupid right now, crying about my damned dog.

"I can't do this; it's making her crazy. She wants to get to me." I turn away. "Let's go upstairs."

Olivia turns the wheelchair around and pushes it to the bottom of the next flight of stairs.

"Are you ready?" My mom asks, standing between the steps and my wheelchair, holding out her hand.

"Yes."

I wipe the tears from my face and push myself up. My mom and sister grab each arm. I shuffle to the first step and grab the railing with my left hand. I slowly make my way to the top, all the while looking in front of me and being careful not to trip and fall. My mom goes ahead of me with a walker. She turns it around, and I grab each side of the walker and push it to the middle of the room just in front of the hospital bed.

My mom had called in advance to have a bed delivered to the house. As much as I would like to sleep in my bedroom upstairs, the climb is too difficult. We had decided that with the hospital bed in the living room, I'd have access to the bathroom and the kitchen. The doctor wants me to be in the hospital bed for at least two months because of the rule of no lifting or twisting.

I push my walker to the edge of the bed and sit down. My mom goes downstairs to park the car, and Olivia goes upstairs. I look around and start to cry again. How did this happen to me? I was supposed to be returning from a productive trip in Indonesia; I was supposed to be coming home to snuggle up on the couch with Dave. Here I am sitting in a hospital bed wondering when I'll get to see my bedroom again, let alone pet my dog. *Why, God?* My breathing is getting heavy and my body is shaking. The tears don't stop.

I push myself up using the walker and turn it to look out the window. I can see the palm trees alongside the edge of the main road and the ocean just out front. The sun is high in the sky and shining. I look down to see London outside sitting by the door, anxiously waiting to be let inside. I am overwhelmed, and sit back down, pushing myself back onto the bed and pulling my legs up. The bed is already in a sitting position, but I grab the remote and adjust it. There are pillows to the side of the bed, next to the wall. I grab two and put them behind me, one at my head and one at my back. I try to sit back more and relax, but the turtle shell cast is in my way. Pushing myself back to the edge of the bed, I stand up holding onto the walker with one hand and using my other hand. I unstrap the cast. Undoing the last strap, the cast falls to the floor with a loud thud.

"Are you okay?" Olivia yells, running down the stairs.

"Yeah, I was just taking off my cast."

She looks down and then walks over to help me back in the bed. She adjusts the pillows and gets me comfortably on my side with a pillow in between my legs.

"I'm tired," I say. "I'm going to take a nap."

**********

I awaken to my sister standing over me. "Anne . . . Anne."

I open my eyes. The room is getting dark; it looks like the sun might be going down.

"It's time for you to take your meds." She hands me some pills and a bottle of water. I put them in my mouth and swallow some water.

"Thanks. How long have I been asleep?"

"A few hours. Mom is upstairs getting ready for bed."

"What time is it?"

"Six o'clock."

"Wow. When does Cruz come back?" I have no sense of time anymore.

"Tomorrow."

"Good. I miss him."

"I'm going to sleep down here on the couch." She points behind my hospital bed. "Do you want me to put a sheet down on it?"

"Yeah, you probably should. It might be more comfortable."

I see a stack of pillows, sheets, and a blanket at the corner of the couch; they were prepared for this.

"Ok, I will. I'm going to set my phone alarm for four hours from now so I can give you your meds—and then every four hours after that, ok?"

"Ok."

"What are you going to want to eat with them? You'll need to eat something so it doesn't hurt your stomach."

"Um, I don't know. I can't think of food right now. You decide."

"I bought some saltine crackers. Is that okay? That's what they were giving you in the hospital."

"No, not those—I am so sick of saltine crackers, if I have to eat one more I'm going to puke!" Before my surgery I loved eating saltine crackers. They reminded me of when I was a little kid at snack time. But now they remind me of the hospital. They'd wake me up in the middle of the night with meds and crackers; sometimes I'd swallow large bites of cracker whole just to get it down.

She laughs. "Yeah, I understand. Are you okay with graham crackers or yogurt?"

"Yeah, that's fine."

She hands me a bottle of water, which I put at my bedside. "Can you turn me? I want to lie on my back."

She walks over and helps me turn over. I had tried earlier but I have no strength. She tucks a couple pillows under my legs to take the pressure off of my spine.

That first night is a rough one; I keep waking up to go to the bathroom or to take meds. Walking to the bathroom isn't an easy task, as I have to wake Olivia up and have her help me push the walker. The bathroom is all set up for me with a commode, a high-chair type of seat set up over the toilet. My legs are weak, so my sister has to pull me up off of the commode and pull my pants up. Once I get back to bed and adjust the pillows again, I'm fully awake. I lie there for what seems like hours, browsing Facebook or texting Dave; he is always very positive and encouraging.

"Here." Olivia wakes me up with some meds in her hand, then she hands me my bottle of water.

"What time is it?" The room is bright and full of light. I use my remote to prop myself up in a sitting position and take the meds.

"Almost eleven—how do you feel?"

"Good. Tired; I didn't sleep very well."

"I know," she laughs.

"How did you sleep?"

"Actually pretty well. I was able to fall back asleep easy every time I woke up with you—and I slept in."

Olivia is one of those people who can't survive without sleep. If she sleeps one hour less, everyone knows it; she ends up being cranky and no fun to be around. When we went to bed last night, I had wondered how she would do. She seems to be looking okay.

"I woke up once at five a.m. when Bridget came to walk London, but I was able to fall back to sleep around six and then didn't wake up until just fifteen minutes ago—so it wasn't too bad."

Bridget had volunteered to take care of London during my recovery. She and her husband have been active in London's life since we brought her home from the breeder, so it's good that London is spending time with someone familiar. Bridget has also been updating everyone in my prayer support group; she has definitely been a huge blessing from God.

"When does Cruz come back? He comes back today, doesn't he?"

"Today. Mom is going to pick him up from school."

"Isn't his last day of school this Friday?" I've been in the hospital most of the month of June and feel like I've missed Cruz's entire school year.

"Yes, and his school program is tomorrow."

"I want to go. I've never missed one."

"Anne, I don't think you should go. It's too dangerous."

"I want to go," I say again stubbornly.

"I'll see if Mom can call the doctor to see if it's okay."

I feel like I could go back to sleep but decide to turn the TV on instead. I don't want to be lazy. My mom brings me a bowl of fresh fruit and a bottle of water. My appetite has increased a little bit, but I am only able to eat a small amount before I am full. I am also dealing with some digestion issues probably relating to all the morphine I am on. The fruit should wash some of it through, as I have never felt so backed up before. "Pooping bricks" is not a term to joke about anymore, as it's a reality for me.

After breakfast, my mom tells me that Bridget has set up an online meal calendar so that people can help out by bringing meals to the house. I think that is a great idea and yet more proof that Bridget is an amazing friend. My mom also tells me that people have been asking her when they can visit, but she has been putting everyone off knowing I don't want visitors. I tell her I will start seeing people tomorrow; I just want to take a shower first. We decide I will only have two visitors a day and that we will start scheduling it now. We go through her list and sadly Rhonda has not reached out yet. I am really bummed but not surprised, because I haven't seen any texts from her, only one comment on a Facebook post I've written. She asked when she could come visit me. Who does that? She's my best friend; we are like sisters. If she really cares, she would have called me or at least texted. Not only do I feel betrayed and hurt, I start to feel angry. While I'm bedridden at home, I see her post pictures partying with other friends, whom I don't know, so I know she is alive and well and has no reason not to check in on me.

My first full day at home consists of watching TV, eating small amounts of food—just enough to take my pills—and plenty of sleep. I wake up when Cruz arrives; it's really nice seeing him at home again, even if it isn't the same. He sits by my bedside and holds my hand; we sit and watch TV together, telling each other "I love you" as many times as we can.

Just before bed, Cruz asks if he can sleep on the couch instead of upstairs in his room. He wants to be close to me. I tell him he won't get any sleep because I have to wake up every four hours to take my meds; he's disappointed but seems to understand. We say our usual prayers and then my mom takes him up to bed.

I stay up a little while longer and end up dozing off.

# pain management

The next morning I can hear Cruz in the kitchen eating breakfast and watching TV. He is being very quiet and whispering from time to time with my mom. I look over at Olivia to see that she is still asleep. The cable box reads almost 8 a.m. I grab my phone connected to the power cord on the side of my bed and see two messages: one from Dave and one from Gavin. I've told both of them they can come and see me when I feel a little better; I don't want to see Gavin until I'm looking much better, but Dave I want to see soon. I miss him a lot.

I look at my calendar to see that Stacy is coming today; it'll be nice to see her. We don't hang out all the time, but when we do, we always have so much fun. We met several years ago when our sons played baseball together, but ever since Cruz stopped playing, we haven't done much. I'm actually surprised she is going to come by.

I hear my mom tell Cruz it's time to go to school, so I close my eyes. I don't want him coming in here and talking to me—he'd for sure wake Olivia up with his voice. I hear him walk up to my bed and then I feel him kiss my head. "I love you, Mom," he whispers and walks down the stairs. I hear my mom following behind with heavy footsteps, and then I hear the garage door close. I open my eyes and look at my phone—right on time for school. Nice.

Soon after, Olivia wakes up to the alarm. She sits up and looks at me while turning it off. "How long have you been awake?"

"Not very long. I heard Cruz getting ready for school and I've been browsing Facebook."

"Oh, good. How do you feel?"

"Not too bad, but a little nauseous. I think it was the yogurt I ate last with the meds."

"Ok. We won't use that again." She gets up off the couch to hand me the meds and some granola.

"Yeah, it's probably better if I eat it during the day when I have other food in my stomach; I've always had issues with dairy."

"Sarah is lactose intolerant. Maybe you are, too?"

"Nah, I'm just sensitive to it from time to time. Hey, can I take a shower this morning?"

"Sure. You must be tired of all that dry shampoo I've been putting in your hair."

Ever since I can remember in the hospital, Olivia has been brushing my hair and putting dry shampoo in it. For the first time ever, I don't care how I look. Olivia has been trying to lift my spirits by doing my hair. I don't even ask; she just does it. That's what family is about.

"You've been doing a great job at doing my hair, Olivia. Thank you," I say with a smile, patting my tangled hair web. "I would just like to wash my body and really shampoo my hair. What has it been—at least a couple weeks, right?"

"Yeah, something like that. Don't worry; we'll get you in the shower today." She smiles.

"Stacy is coming around noon. Can we do it early?"

"Sure, as soon as I'm done drinking my coffee. We'll go upstairs."

The walk upstairs is difficult and yet delightful. Walking past my office is tough, and looking down at my desk, seeing things stacked up on it, waiting for my time, is also hard. When we step into my bedroom, the memories come rushing back. The last time I saw this room I was excited and anxious about traveling to Indonesia, thinking I would come back to sleep in my bed just before taking off to Vegas the night I returned. Amazing how things can change at the blink of an eye. Now my room is consumed with my mom's suitcase and her clothes are scattered around the room.

I use the walker to get to the shower, going past my closet. I look down in the closet to see my already packed suitcase waiting for my return from Indo and the girls' trip to Vegas. I stand at the shower door looking in. How sad this is. There are towels on the floor of the shower—my mom had put them there so I don't slip—and the commode is in the middle of the floor.

Olivia turns on the water. "We are supposed to be careful and not get water directly on your bandages, but we'll change them after the shower, so don't worry too much."

*This is weird*, I think to myself. I will have to get completely naked in front of my sister. I slowly start to take off my shirt. Unable to do it myself, Olivia helps me lift it over my head. I can't bend over to pull down my shorts, so she pulls them off. I am standing there in my bathroom, completely naked. Awkward.

I get into the shower. It feels nice, the warm water running across my hands. I slowly sit in the chair, and Olivia hands me a clear plastic container to pour water on my body. The chair is directly in the water's path in order to keep the water from hitting me in the face. Olivia starts to brush out my hair, which is a tangled mess. Soon she pours water on my head and starts to wash my hair. I am unable to reach to my head yet with my arms, so she will have to do everything. It feels good to have her wash my hair, but I'm also feeling lifeless. Having my own sister bathe me is surreal. Never in a lifetime had I thought this would be happening. She continues to wash my entire body, feet, legs, arms—she even shaves my legs when I ask her. She doesn't even blink. This must be weird for her, too.

When the shower is all done, I carefully step out and sit on the edge of the tub while she dries me off. Again, because I can't bend or twist, I'm unable to do anything. Olivia helps me get dressed, and she works on putting a new bandage on my back and side. It doesn't hurt, but the pain starts to creep back in after standing in front of the mirror for a while. She takes me back downstairs and gives me more meds. I realize at this point that I need to time my showers just after taking my pain meds, when they're at peak performance. I sit in bed while Olivia brushes out my hair, which is getting long. I rest for a little bit and then put some make-up on—just a bit of powder and blush, enough so I don't look so pale. I haven't been in the sun now for a month.

That afternoon, Stacy comes by with a huge vase of beautiful flowers. She pulls up a chair next to my bed and starts to cry. "Anne, I can't believe this happened to you. Seeing you in this hospital bed is killing me. Tell me what happened."

I tell her the story and she starts to cry again, this time unable to talk. I sit there looking at her, trying to feel what she's feeling, trying to feel some sort of emotion, but I can't. Why does this keep happening?

"Anne, oh my gosh—you could have drowned. You're lucky you came up out of that water! God had his hands on you, that's for sure!"

"Yeah, I know—scary."

"Anne! Cruz almost lost his mom! Oh my!" She's wiping the tears from her face as fast as they're falling. "You could have been paralyzed. What a miracle you are—and still so pretty." She's now trying to make light of all she just said, seeing how serious this is.

"Yeah, that's what the doctors say."

"Seriously, God kept you here on earth for a reason, Anne. You need to figure that out." Her tears start to slow down. "Maybe God did this so that you might meet a handsome doctor and live happily ever after!" We both laugh.

"Yeah, but my doctor is married!"

"Oh . . . Well, then, maybe your physical therapist!"

We laugh again. "I'm sure there is a reason behind all of this."

We chat for a while longer, and then she leaves to go home after giving me a hug and praying for me. Up until this point I haven't realized how spiritual she is; I guess God has a reason for everything. Soon after Stacy leaves, my mom comes home and enters my room to tell me that the doctor approved my field trip to see the school program. He said I need to stay in the wheelchair the entire time, and if I start to feel pain, I need to go home. I'm thrilled to be able to go.

I lie down for a nap; the visit with Stacy and the shower earlier have worn me out.

**********

I want to surprise Cruz, so I've asked Jeff to take him to the school early. My mom and Olivia get me ready. Wearing the turtle shell, I carefully enter the passenger side of my car, with a pillow behind my back. I'm all set to go. My mom drives slowly, being sure not to jar my back with any bounces. I called the school office earlier to inform them I would be coming and had asked if they would set aside a chair close to the door and in front for me. They obliged and told me they had all been praying for me.

We pull up to the school and luckily get a parking spot up close to the front doors. Olivia comes around with the wheelchair and opens my door. *Okay*, I think to myself, *this is going to be humbling—being wheeled into Cruz's school sitting in a wheel chair, looking like death*. Not only have I lost fifteen pounds, I've lost my tan and am now pale. My mom helps me out of the car and into the wheelchair. People are walking by and looking at me; some pretend not to see me and some do the half-smile. The half-smile is when they acknowledge you, but they feel bad for you because you're in a wheelchair.

My mom pushes me towards the doors, but I ask her to stop because I see some of Cruz's friends playing on the grass. They must know I'm looking at them because they all stop to stare, and then one of them yells out, "Hi, Miss Latour!" Just then Cruz comes running out and leans over the chair to hug me.

"Mom! You're here!"

"Yes, I wanted it to be a surprise."

He smiles a smile I haven't seen in ages. He looks very proud.

"I gotta' go—see you after," he says, and runs into the building with all the other kids.

My mom pushes my wheelchair into the school, and as soon as we enter, we see three seats with my name on them. I just want to cry, this is so nice. Olivia moves one of the chairs so we can fit the wheelchair in and then they sit down. I look around to see that everyone is staring at me; there are some familiar faces and some new faces. Just then the show starts.

It's a great performance; I'm unable to see Cruz from where I'm sitting, but just to be there is a blessing. When it concludes, I'm bombarded by friends giving me hugs and wishing me well. Some people even come up to tell me they've heard what happened and have been praying for me, even though they personally don't know me. It is just amazing to see the outpouring of support from the school. I've known the principal even before Cruz started here—she was an old neighbor of mine—but I never expected this much love and support.

That night I go to sleep in my hospital bed in the middle of my living room—feeling very loved.

**********

The following morning I wake up in extreme pain. My right arm is hurting, and I am feeling a massive amount of pressure and sharp pain just under my right breast. My mom calls the doctor and they say to come in right away. The ride to the doctor's office is rough, but we make it. It's the first time I get to see where my doctor works; it is a nice big office and very high-tech. Doctor Donnald isn't in, but his other physician assistant comes in to see me. After looking at my arm, she tells me to go next door, back to the hospital to have my arm checked out. My arm is discolored with bruises from the IVs that were placed in my arm during my hospital stay. She is concerned that I might have a blood clot, which could be dangerous, considering what my body has already gone through. She also looks at my rib cage, where I'm having the other pain. After doing some poking around, she tells me I am still swollen, but wants to refer me to a neurologist.

My mom drives the car around to the entrance of the hospital, bypassing the emergency room. As we pass the ER entrance, I realize that's where it all began here in the States. Memories come flooding back and I start to tear up. *Why, God?* My mom stops at the entrance to the hospital; Olivia gets out, helping me into a wheelchair. The hospital staff comes over immediately to help us. I get checked in and brought to the back. I guess telling them that I could have a potential blood clot from a surgery done there helps motivate them. After waiting for a short period of time, a doctor comes in to exam me. Seeing my brace and the state I am in, I'm sure I don't look like I belong there, but upstairs in a hospital room. He tells me he will have an ultrasound done as soon as possible, and try to get me out of there soon. After waiting a couple hours, the radiologist comes in to see me. She is pushing a cart with equipment and looks exhausted.

"Hello. I'm Dr. Kang," she says, walking into the room. "I'm here to see if you have a blood clot."

"Yes, we've been waiting for a while and I'm in a hurry to get home. I've spent enough time in hospitals." I'm sitting in the wheelchair, with my turtle shell brace, covered in blankets.

"Oh, I see. What happened to you?"

I tell her the story and then explain that I have been in pain from the IVs. I also add that I don't want to spend another night in the hospital and that if they find anything wrong, to please take care of it and let me go home today.

"I think I heard about you—you're the Bali girl, right?"

I laugh, "Yeah, that's me. Were you here the night I came in?"

"No, but everyone was talking about it—you're a tough girl."

"Thanks." I smile.

She helps me get up on the gurney with a step stool and then starts the ultrasound. It takes one hour; she has to start at my hand and go up my arm, shoulder, neck, and chest. She takes several still images and seems to focus on certain areas, taking notes. When she finishes, she tells me there are some clots she is concerned with, but she needs a second opinion. An hour later, another doctor walks in with a piece of paper.

"Anne?"

"Yes, that's me—the one in the turtle shell cast." I'm lying on the gurney, covered in blankets, dozing off. This has been a long and exhausting day for me, mentally and physically.

"You have four blood clots."

Those words hit me like a ton of bricks. "What does that mean? Do I have to be admitted?" I don't want to spend another minute in this hospital, let alone another night; the color drains from my face as all my hopes vanish of going home to my hospital bed.

"Well . . ." he pauses, "No, we called a specialist and your doctor—they both think we can let you go home. You will need to apply heat to your arm and take this prescription for two days." He's holding up the prescription. "It should start feeling better tomorrow. If it doesn't, let us know as soon as possible, okay?"

"Thank you! Thank you!" I say excitedly. Yes, there is a God—I get to go home.

We check out of the hospital and head home, picking Cruz up from school on the way. He is excited to see me in the car, as I am to see him. It's nice having him around; he is the fresh air, the young energy that brings smiles to my face and hope into my life.

That evening, Cruz sits next to my hospital bed holding my hand and watching TV. I start to feel better with the heating packs and meds, but still on my mind is the pain in my rib cage. My twin sister told me over the phone that it could be gallbladder problems, which would make sense with all the meds I've been on. I don't want to think about it, so I push it from my mind—I'll let the doctor deal with it.

I don't sleep very well that night, waking up in extreme pain under my breast. Every time I press on it, I feel pressure. Thankfully my arm feels better. If it's not one thing, it's another. I feel bad because it's Olivia's last night with me; she doesn't sleep much, either, as I keep getting up to go to the bathroom or need to be turned.

The following morning, my mom and Cruz leave to take Olivia to the airport and pick up my twin sister Sarah. Olivia needs to get back home to her husband and follow up on the family business. With Olivia's departure, my twin sister has volunteered to come down to help my mom out. It's been a huge strain on my mom, taking care of me and helping out with Cruz. If she were thirty years younger, it wouldn't be an issue.

Just as my mom pulls out of the garage, I hear Carrie's voice. "*Yoo-hoo! Yoo-hoo!*"

I sit up on my bed and look over the railing into the pool table room. What's Carrie doing here? "Carrie?"

"Hi, honey. I'm here to babysit you." She laughs as she walks up the stairs.

"Seriously?" I laugh and try to fix my hair; I must look like crap.

"Yes. Sorry, but your mom called me and asked if I'd come over while she takes Olivia to the airport." She sits down on a step stool next to my bed. "I think she's worried you might try going upstairs to your bedroom or start cleaning."

I laugh, "Oh my God! My mom is driving me crazy! She doesn't trust me!"

"So . . . I know this mess has got to be killing you," she says, looking around. There are piles of papers and dead flowers everywhere.

"Yes!" I slowly push myself to the edge of the bed.

"Ok, this is what we are going to do," she says with a big smile. "We are going to clean this mess up, throw out the dead flowers—and get you some sun!"

"Really?"

"Yes! I know you are dying to get some sun and it must be so hard on you, so as soon as we get this place cleaned up, we'll go downstairs and sit outside."

She starts bustling around the house organizing things and throwing out dead flowers, asking from time to time if I want to keep a pot. When it's all done, she comes over to me holding the walker. "Ok, are you ready?"

"Never more ready." I get up and push the walker to the door.

"You have to promise me not to tell your mom!" She helps me step by step down the stairs.

"Don't worry—I'd never tell her!"

We get to the bottom and she grabs a step stool to put outside. Slowly she helps me walk through the front doors and into the sun. The rays hit me like a shower of warm water; the sun is bright and high in the sky. I've forgotten this feeling. Carrie helps me sit down in the middle of the walkway, directly in the sunlight.

"Thank you for thinking about this, Carrie; I'd given up on seeing and feeling the sunlight."

We sit there for thirty minutes, just enough to feel like I'm getting high from the heat and vitamin D. She then helps me back upstairs into the living room and into my hospital bed.

Just then I hear my twin sister and mom downstairs in the garage. Carrie and I look at each other and laugh. "Perfect timing!" I say.

"Love you, sweetie." She gives me a gentle hug. "Gotta' go!"

I can hear her say something to my mom and sister and then shut the door. I look over the railing to see Sarah standing in the pool table room, looking at London. There is a baby gate separating her from the rest of the house.

"Don't worry, she won't hurt you!" I yell down to her. She looks up and smiles. "Yeah, but she looks like she could kill me."

"She wouldn't hurt a fly." I scoot to the edge of my bed, ready to give her a hug. Sarah hasn't been down here to SoCal since I got married. For her to be here right now is a big deal.

She comes up the stairs, wearing her purple fleece jacket and blue jeans, carrying a large suitcase and small brown bag. I pull my walker over and stand up, and she comes over and hugs me. "Anne, I am so glad you are okay."

"Thank you for coming all the way down here . . . for me."

"Of course I'd come help you!"

She steps back and takes off her jacket. "How are you feeling?"

"I have a lot of pain right here." I point to my rib cage under my breast. She touches it, pressing against it. "It's really swollen—looks like blood has pooled right here." Although she's not a doctor, she seems to know a lot about the body. "Do you have an appointment with the doctor yet?"

"Yes, Monday."

"Good—only two more days."

"How's the pain? Are you ready to start weaning yourself from the meds?"

"I don't have any pain as long as I take my meds on time. Luckily, I've been doing really well with it. Olivia surprised me; she was a huge help!" I sit back down on the bed and scoot back. "I have a Fentanyl patch on and I take morphine every four hours."

"Wow, Anne—morphine?"

"Yep."

"That is so not good for you. We are going to get you off of that!"

"I know, but it works. I think I was on so much meds in Indonesia that my tolerance level is different."

"Don't worry," she laughs. "I'll help you get off of it."

The weekend consists of watching TV and lying low. Sarah is trying to make the best of her vacation time and I'm struggling with the pain. At one point Sarah takes London for a run on the beach and ends up calling my mom to pick her up because London can't run back home the six miles she has already run. Sarah is in really good shape, ready for her Tough Mudder competition the following week. The Tough Mudder is a competition for people who want to challenge themselves physically through obstacle courses while raising money for a good cause. Seeing her head out for her runs every day is hard on me. Here I am sitting in my hospital bed, waiting for the go ahead from my doctor to start taking walks. Having her here is truly humbling.

Monday morning rolls around not soon enough. Sarah stays home with Cruz, saying that she's going to teach him how to be more responsible by doing chores around the house while my mom takes me to see the doctor.

We get to the doctor's office and fill out all the paper work. Shortly after, a nurse calls me up. She leads us back to a small patient room and we sit down. By this time, I am able to walk without the walker as long as my mom stays nearby just in case I lose my balance and fall.

The doctor, a tall Asian man in his sixties, walks in and introduces himself. He asks if I am the Bali girl, and I tell him the story.

"How are you doing? How's the recovery been?"

"Horrible. I am in a lot of pain." I point to my ribs.

He has me pull my shirt up and looks closely at it. Then he uses a couple different tools on his counter to touch my skin where the pain is.

"Do you feel this?"

"Sort of; it feels like pressure."

"How about this?"

"OW!" I jump. It feels like a million needles.

"This?" He uses something else and runs it along my back toward my ribs.

"Yeah, pressure— oh, wait, I didn't feel it . . . OW!"

He stands back and pulls my shirt down. "You have nerve damage at the thoracic ten."

Now I've heard some really bad news this past month, but this one— this one hit me the hardest. I've heard of people having nerve damage; it lasts forever and never improves. If the doctor accidentally damaged a nerve during surgery, I'm screwed.

"What? Nerve damage? What does that mean?"

"Well, it happens to the best of doctors; they can't always see the nerves."

"So what does this mean? Will I ever get back to normal?"

"The chances are slim. There are some radical new therapies and research being done every day for nerve damage. Here." He hands me a piece of paper with a website on it.

"So . . ." Tears fill my eyes. I am trying to be strong for my mom—and for myself as well. "Will I always have this pain? Every time I put a shirt on, every time I touch it?"

"Hard to say. It's still early." He sits down on his stool. "I can do a nerve block injection, but I think we should wait a few weeks on that. In the meantime, you can take Lyrica for the pain. I'll give you some samples to take home with you."

I am still trying to be strong, but now the reality is setting in—nerve blockers—Lyrica—all just to have a normal life. Right now, there is no way I can go on with this pain. Every time I move and my shirt rubs against me, or I hug someone, I feel it—and the thought of being intimate with a man is terrifying.

We leave the doctor's office and head home. The entire drive, I look out my window with tears rolling down my face. I can't bring myself to say anything. My mom chats about how giving it to God would be good for me and that everything happens for a reason. Sometimes I get tired of hearing her preach to me—as if I don't believe that He's my God, too.

Once home, Sarah tells me I shouldn't take the Lyrica because of the side effects; she suggests waiting out the pain for a few more weeks to see if my body heals itself. I just nod my head in disbelief and crawl into bed. Just then Cruz comes downstairs from his shower.

"Mom," he leans in to whisper in my ear, "Can I snuggle with you?"

"I'm sorry, honey, but not yet." Grabbing his hand, I look at him. "I know you want to, and I miss our snuggle time, but it's too dangerous with my side incision—and I have a lot of pain right here." I point at my ribcage.

"I promise to be careful." He has tears in his eyes, so I look away, trying not to cry, too.

"I'm sorry, bud; you can't."

"Mom, I miss things the way they were . . . I wish everything would just go back to normal."

At this point, I can no longer hold my tears back. "Oh, honey," I grab onto him and pull him tight to my side, "So do I . . . So do I." We hold each other and cry for a while. I forget how this must be so hard on him, all these people coming in and out of his house every day visiting and bringing meals; his life has turned upside down and it is completely out of my control.

That night when everyone goes to sleep—my mom in my bedroom, Cruz in his, and Sarah on the couch next to me—I decide to have a meeting with God. All of this time, from the moment I broke my back until now, I have taken Him for granted. I acknowledge Him when people say I am a miracle, and I acknowledge Him when people say they've been praying for me—but not once have I had a conversation with Him since I left for my missions trip. I lie there looking up at the ceiling lit by the moonlight . . .

*God, if you're there—I am sorry. I am sorry for not coming to You sooner—but I need You right now, more than ever. You have protected me this entire time, from death and from paralysis—and I haven't thanked You. Thank You, God. Thank You for giving me another opportunity at life. Thank You for saving my family from burying me. Thank you.*

**********

131

That morning, the very first thing I do is open my devotional. From this day forward, I vow to myself, I will put God first in my life.

"Mom?"

I look up to see Cruz standing next to my bed; I've just set aside my Bible. "Yeah, bud?"

"My dad's here; it's time for me to go."

I forgot he is going back to his dad's today. "Shoot, I forgot. Ok, bud. I love you."

He gives me a hug. "I love you, too, Mom." He grabs his back pack and walks down the stairs. I hear him say good-bye to London, and then the door shuts.

I lie back in my bed, adjusting the pillows around me. Closing my eyes, I think about Cruz—oh, how I'll miss him. Tears fill my eyes. He's been the light of my life; I love having him around. God, I'm going to miss him. What am I going to do without him for the next six days? Now tears are flowing down my cheeks. His little laughter and his loving gestures, always grabbing my hand and kissing it, telling me he loves me . . . And here I am stuck in this damned hospital bed, with the same boring schedule, lying here watching TV, looking at my laptop and wondering what my day will be like—pain or no pain. I sure do miss my life. *God, I know You have greater plans for me, but this is hard.*

I can't stop crying. I feel so alone and out of control. "Damn it!" I hit the pillow and feel the anger well up inside. My throat is knotted and my ears are burning.

*This isn't fair, God. Why? I remember waking up on Sunday mornings, lying in my bed debating which to do first: the gym or coffee. And on bad days, on days I felt everything was going wrong, I would lie there asking You why You can't bring a man into my life, a man to wake up with. Now I'm lying here wondering why I'm waking up in a hospital bed.*

# getting through it

The next several weeks consist of watching TV and having visitors. Sarah has gone home after one week, and it's just my mom and I. Rhonda still hasn't reached out to me, so I have given up hope that she ever will. Knowing her, she'll probably wait until I'm better. I'm starting to realize that maybe I was just her party friend, although she had said I was like a sister to her. She obviously hadn't meant it; sisters don't just disappear like this. I am hurt. I feel like I lost my best friend when I jumped off that cliff. Probably the best thing about this, though, is that I have realized who truly is a friend of mine. I've had friends reach out to me whom I haven't spoken to in more than a year; even friends of friends are stepping up and reaching out to me.

One of the best evenings is when my friend Cindy brings sushi over and helps my mom do laundry. Cindy is a beautiful, six-foot-tall brunette with such a soft heart. I've known her since Cruz was a baby. We met at a mothers' play group and have been close friends ever since. Cindy and I chat as if nothing has happened; I think she knows I need a break from reality.

The following evening, Dave calls to say he is stopping by. Although we've been texting every day, I haven't seen him since I left for my trip to Indonesia. He has told me that he recently got a tattoo of his parents on his back and he wants to show me. I know his parents mean a lot to him, so it doesn't surprise me that he went to such an extreme. Plus, ever since he's gone back to college, he's been acting a bit different.

My mom has already gone to bed when Dave shows up. I'm not feeling all that great about his coming by so late. I don't want him to think anything is going to happen. Ever since I've made my vow to put God first several weeks ago, things have been changing for the good in my life. The nerve pain has subsided and the swelling has disappeared. I wonder now if God is testing me, checking to see if I can handle myself around Dave, even after putting God first.

Before I left for Indonesia, I thought I had the closest relationship with God I've ever had in years. I was straightening out my life, cleaning up the music I listened to, spending more time in prayer, going to church every week. I felt so close to God that I even felt His calling to go on that missions trip. Everything seemed so perfect in my life, seemed like it was all lining up—but there was still one thing I wasn't ready to give over to God, and that was my relationship with Dave. Although God had told me to stop the sexual activity, and although I had stopped it with other men, I hadn't done so with Dave. I kept making excuses: *we have such a strong connection; I've never felt this with anyone else; he's a Christian; he cares for me; he loves me* . . . I had so many excuses—and of course there was the famous one: *next time I'll stand my ground and tell him no.*

Now that I'm going to see him in person for the first time since everything happened, I'm scared. He shows up as normal, calling from the garage telling me he's here. Since I can't go down the stairs to open the door, I tell him the garage code and to let himself in. When he walks into the room, I melt. I get up and give him a hug. Feeling his arms wrap around my body is like a dream; it feels so good, so comforting. He helps me sit down on my bed and then hands me a bag he brought with him. Inside is full of magazines and candy, my favorite kind.

We talk for a while, and then he shows me his tattoo. It's still scabbing and a little bloody; he's just had it done several days ago. As I run my fingers along the drawing and down his back, I so badly want to kiss it, but I hold back, thinking about the jump and about my broken back. Part of me wonders if God has allowed this because of my disobedience to Him.

"It looks really good," I say, patting him on his shoulder, as if to say, *Okay—I'm done admiring it.*

He puts his shirt back on and turns to me, touches my face, and kisses me. His lips are soft on my mouth, so tender . . . Electricity runs through my body, as if to say, *you know you want it.* Just as I kiss him back, I hear a voice: *Anne, is this really what you want? Was all that for nothing?*

After kissing him one more time, I push Dave away. "We shouldn't do this."

"It's okay. I understand." He gets up. "I need to go anyway."

I walk him to the edge of the stairs and he leans over to kiss me goodbye. I accept and give him a hug. "Thank you for everything. Seriously, you are a great friend."

He hugs me and walks out. I lie back in my bed and pray. *God, thank You for giving me the willpower to stop anything from happening.*

That night I fall asleep, happy and content. For the first time ever, I feel more in control of my life.

**********

The next day I get bad news: A letter from my landlord states that I need to move out within sixty days or I will be evicted. I spend all morning trying to get a hold of him. I have been living here for six years now and we've had a great relationship; it doesn't make sense that he's asking me to leave. He doesn't answer his phone or his emails, so I call my neighbor. He tells me he has just seen him at a board meeting, and that he told him about my injury. After discussing it a while, we conclude that it could be the reason he is asking me to leave—he's hoping to avoid evicting me if I can't pay my rent. I call my attorney, who tells me that since we don't have a lease, I have no recourse.

I hang up the phone and sit there in my hospital bed looking at the phone. *God—really? Did you think I was handling everything else so well that You have to go and throw this at me?* I look out the window. This place has been home to me for so many years, and there are so many memories here. *Why, God? Why are you doing this to me? Why? Have I done something wrong? Am I living my life in such a way that You don't want me to continue the way I'm living? I'm sorry, God; I'm so sorry. I know I have to thank You for this, for everything You've put in my life—but this is hard. I've lost everything as I've known it—my lifestyle and my best friend—and now I have to move. Why do You have to make it worse and uproot me during the hardest time in my life?*

That week I call every realtor I know, asking them to keep an eye out for me. I look online and see nothing but old, broken down rental homes. I'm starting to panic when my friend Jack comes to see me.

Jack tells me to stay in the present. He teaches me how to relax and see things as they are right now. "You're alive, right?"

"Yeah."

"You're walking?"

"Yeah."

"You have a roof over your head right now, yeah?"

"Yeah."

"Well, then, everything is great, right now—in the present!" He smiles.

"Yeah, you're right."

"Of course I am," he says and laughs. "Anne, you have your faith in God. Have faith that God will work everything out for you."

"You're right. This is all part of His plan."

Still, it's hard to accept these difficulties and these curves God keeps throwing at me. I continue to trust that this is all part of His plan. True, I'm not where I want to be in life, but are we ever where we want to be in life? As I've gone through these past months, I've had time to think about that. We will never get to exactly where we want because we will always want more. We are built that way, striving to succeed just a little bit more, whether it's our family life, our career, our possessions, our friends. We will always want more; it's in our DNA. Look at Adam and Eve; from the beginning of time humans have always wanted more. We are always looking on the other side of the fence. Ask yourself, do you have a roof over your head? Can you feed yourself? Are you able to have a relationship with God? If so, you don't need much more. Everything else is a plus.

**\*\*\*\*\*\*\*\*\***

I wake up to London's barking. She's probably scaring the heck out of another neighbor. I laugh to myself, and turn to see that it's eight-thirty. I stare at the ceiling, and my mind starts to race into the past. I sit up, take a gulp of water, and grab my devotional. Today's message is about letting God's love seep into my inner self, into the deepest part of my being where I try to keep secrets from Him. If I try to keep secrets from God, then those secrets will become worms and wiggle through my life developing lives of their own, controlling me without even realizing it. Amazingly enough, that is what has happened to me. I read it a second and third time. I put it down and sit silently, meditating on the words.

*God, I'm putting this out there to You because I don't want any secrets. I am afraid of being homeless; please help me overcome my fear.*

When I was a child, my dad went through a tough transition in his career; he had quit his job without planning ahead. We had a rough Christmas I never forgot—but the hardest part about it was watching my mom open up a cardboard box of donations that someone from the church had dropped off. I remember my mom trying to keep the tears from falling down her cheeks as she pulled each item from the box. Even though she said nothing, I knew it was hard on her pride to have to depend on someone else to feed her kids. That has stuck with me and scares me almost every day. I don't want to put Cruz through anything close to that—not that we are homeless, but the thought of not being able to provide for my son scares the life right out of me.

I breathe in and out. *God, I have a problem with sex.* I know it's not right to have sex with someone I am not married to, but ever since my emotional and physical connection with Dave, I have searched for it and done many wrongs in trying to find it. Satan has used it to create a connection with Dave that continues to lead to my failing promises to You to stay pure. Although I know God has promised the right man for me will come around, I stumble at times—especially when I am around Dave. I have a weakness for him that I cannot control. *God, please let your love seep deep into my soul killing that addiction; help me stay strong to Your words when I am around him.*

I meditate a while longer before getting up to prepare for the day ahead of me. I wash my face and throw a black, long-sleeved shirt on and some pink shorts. As I walk downstairs, I can smell Mom's cooking coming from the kitchen. Oh, how I love her cooking.

"Good morning," she says. "I'm making crepes."

I walk over and grab my turtle brace from the sofa. "My favorite," I say as I'm strapping myself into the brace. It gets easier every time.

"How did you sleep, Mom?" I sit down at the table.

"I slept in an hour later than normal. How about you?"

"Incredibly well. I only woke up once to take my meds."

After breakfast I sit down to think about the day ahead of me; my phone rings and I look down to see it's Dave calling.

"Hey, there." I listen for his voice on the other end.

"What's up, Miss? I just landed." There's a slight pause. "Thought I'd come through, if you're around."

I think quickly. I haven't made any plans yet, so if he comes by for a little while, that would be okay. "Sure. I'm around."

"I know you got Lil' Man and all, plus your mom is there, so I don't want to bother you all." I roll my eyes; he knows it's okay to come by when they're here.

"Cruz is at his dad's, and my mom's about to lie down for a nap."

I can hear the airport hustle and bustle in the background. "I just got that tattoo touched up—you know, the one of my parents. Do you think you can help me clean it?"

I look at the time. It's almost noon. "Of course I'll help you. Come on by." I hang up the phone. *God, please give me the strength to be strong when I see him. God let your love seep deep within me.*

He shows up about thirty minutes later, bag in hand and wearing a black t-shirt and grey shorts. "Hey, Miss," he says as he leans over and kisses me ever so gently on the lips. We walk upstairs and he sets his bag down next to the couch. I'm feeling at peace with him in the house; my heart isn't jumping into my throat, thank God.

"So, how have you been?" he asks.

"Good—just stuck here day after day, doing much of nothing," I reply.

"That's what you should be doing. You gotta' let your body heal," he chuckles as he opens his bag.

I laugh. "It's boring, though—drives me crazy."

He grabs a bar of soap and a small white tube. "Come on, I'll need you to wash my back in the shower. You'll need to wash it and then wipe this ointment on it after I dry off."

I follow him up the stairs to my bedroom. *Damn*, I'm thinking; *really, a shower?* The last time I took a shower with him, good things did not come from it.

I turn the shower on for him and make sure it's not too hot; he's always had problems adjusting the water temperature in my bathroom. "Don't worry," I say, closing the door. "It's not too hot; I know you don't like it as hot as I do." I chuckle. In my experience, guys don't seem to like the shower water as warm as women do.

He gets in and closes the door. I think to myself that I hope he doesn't expect me to get in there. I go in my bedroom and change into a tank top so as not to get wet while washing his back. I return, open the shower stall door, and start washing down his back. I'm not much for tattoos, but it sure looks nice. I'm rubbing the soap all over his back thinking that normally this would get me in trouble, but I'm not going to let it happen this time. He rinses off and steps out of the shower. Boy, does he look good; it looks as if he's been working out. I say a little prayer.

He dries off and stands naked in front of me. I start to tend to his tattoo. I can see the tense bits of pain in his face as I'm touching his back, and I can feel it in mine. I'll never forget those times when my sister had to take off the bandages and clean my stitches, the stinging tinges of pain and the tightness of my muscles.

I finish up and sit down on the bed as he walks back to the bedroom and starts to put lotion on his body, careful not to touch the tattoo. I keep my eyes on his face or otherwise look around, so as not to get aroused.

He sits down next to me and leans in, saying, "Thank you for helping me." He kisses me, and I find myself kissing him back. *Oh no, this is not good* . . . We are sitting here on my bed kissing after a shower. Every time this happens, I end up breaking my promise to God. *Please, God, help me to be strong and say no if the time arises.* Dave continues to gently kiss me and leans me back onto my bed, his hand slowly roaming.

"Dave," I whisper, "No, I don't . . . Umm, I can't."

I pause and lick my lips. "I'm going on this journey and . . ."

He touches my lips ever so gently. "I just wanted to say thank you." He props himself up half-way while I lie flat beside him. "It's ok; you don't need to say any more." He kisses me one last time before getting up. I can see that he's disappointed, but he needs to understand that we can no longer be what we were. He knows I want to be in a committed relationship, and if he doesn't want the same, he needs to man up and step out.

God has put me through so much to wake me up out of the nonsense life I was living; there is no way I am going back to that—not after all I have been through.

There's kind of a weird stale silence, so I try to break it. "I love the tat, and it looks really cool."

He gets up and puts his shirt on. "Thanks, Miss."

As we walk down the stairs, I say a silent thank you to God.

Dave grabs the rest of his stuff and gives me a hug good-bye. "I'll check in with you tomorrow; maybe you can help me clean it again."

I'm carefully hugging him back. "Definitely. Let me know if you need me."

I gently let him go and he turns to walk down the steps.

After the door closes behind him, I sit down on the hospital bed and sigh. That was a close one. I'm going to have to talk to him and really let him know that what we've been doing needs to end if he can't commit. I am looking for my best friend, my companion, my sexual monster—but it has to be with God's rules. He will need to commit only to me. I know God wants more for me. I know God has that person for me, and if it's not Dave, then I have to be available for the man God has planned for me. I lie back on my hospital bed and sigh again. If I don't have that conversation with him, I am doing a disservice to myself and to God. Dave will need to know I'm on a new journey of faith, hoping to find my true love.

**********

The following day, I decide to take a look at a rental I see listed online. Although I am still wearing my brace, I decide to take the chance and venture out to see it. My mom drives me to the house. It is a two-story detached home with a yard. This should be great for London. We walk inside, just as a prospect is leaving.

The home is a little older than I'm used to, but it has charm. The kitchen has a cute nook with large glass windows, which would be a perfect place to grow herbs. The yard is really big with grass from fence to fence. But the best part about it is that one of the bedrooms has a loft with a ladder—Cruz would love it.

I ask for an application and tell the realtor I'm fairly sure I'll want it. Up until this point I have viewed much smaller and older homes. This one isn't exactly what I'm looking for, but it might work. I'll have to pray about it.

Knowing that I have to be moving out in two weeks, I talk my mom into letting me sleep in my bedroom. I have mixed feelings about ever sleeping in my room again, but part of me thinks I would regret it if I don't before I move out. I've been in my hospital bed for two months now, so it's going to be a bit different having to push myself up out of bed, but I think I can do it.

I go into my powder room to grab all of my things. I'm standing there thinking that every time I go up to that room, my heart skips a beat; they contain all of the reminders of how my life used to be—especially the memories of spending time with Dave there. I'll never forget the time when he had come back from a long trip and wasn't feeling well. I had placed scented candles alongside each hardwood step throughout my house. At the top of the stairs in my bedroom, I had a pot of tea and a white sheet spread across my bed. I had topped it with scattered pink, red, and yellow roses. What a time I'll never forget. Or that time I was getting ready to go out for a girls' night with my friend Rhonda, who sat on my bed drinking her vodka, talking about our fun-filled adventures to come while I was finishing my make-up.

*So many memories.* I stand in the bathroom and reach for my black bag that I've been living out of the past two months. My heart starts to race, and I feel faint. I take a deep breath and tell myself to live in the now, to stay in the present. I walk up the stairs feeling a cold sweat sweep over my body; my legs are shaking and my breath is shallow. My heart feels like it's going to jump out of my chest. I don't like this feeling. What if I can't handle the memories?

I enter my bedroom and sit on the bed; the memories start to flood my head—especially ones with Dave. *God, please help me; please give me the strength to get through this. You have gotten me through every day and every obstacle to this point; please just get me through the first night.* Big breath. *Please help me overcome the fears of remembering the past. I know it will not just be tonight, but every night I sleep in this bed moving forward.*

As I head back downstairs, it's already time to leave for church. We've decided to do the Saturday evening service because it's the pastor's first time back after sixteen weeks since his son's death. His twenty-seven-year-old son had taken his own life after struggling with a mental disorder. With several network stations planning on attending, this will be a powerful message I don't want to miss. We pull up to the church and it is jammed packed with cars and network vans and people everywhere. We find my friends who have already been waiting to get in. The church doors open, and everyone scatters for a good seat. We get lucky and sit five rows from the front, directly centered from the pulpit. God sure was looking out for us; this couldn't have been a more perfect location. As the service starts, I can feel the love of God surrounding me. The former tense feelings I had about sleeping in my room are melting away. God is good. After some praise and worship, the pastor comes up and offers one of the most powerful sermons I've heard in years. What an amazing spirit he has. The sermon is called "Getting Through What You Go Through." It hits the nail right on the head for me, after all I've been through, losing my dad and breaking my back. This is exactly what I need.

We drive home on a high. My mom and I speak very little, but I know we are both thinking about the sermon, running it in our minds over and over making sure not to miss a single word. Street lights and the traffic from the local county fair can't touch us; nothing bothers us. I feel God's embrace and God's peace all around me. As we pull into the garage, I look at my mom and say that I'm very tired and want to go to bed; she doesn't complain, and we both head upstairs for our separate bedrooms, she in my son's room, and I in my room for the very first night.

I lie there thinking about the sermon, and what a gift it is to have been there. I am so blessed to have had the chance to hear the pastor speak on such an incredible night. The pastor spoke of staying strong through life's battles, and how to have peace when things don't make sense. One of the things that sticks out in my mind is that having the answer to why this happened to me won't solve anything. My back will still be broken, the pain will still be real, and life's challenges ahead of me will always be there. Explanations to questions don't help; knowing why won't make it better. What I need to do is lean on God. Life won't make sense, but I can have peace because I know that God is with me and He loves me. As it says in the Bible, "I will never leave you and I will never abandon you." It goes on to say, "When you go through deep waters, I will be with you. When you pass through rivers of difficulty, you will not drown. When you walk through the fire, you will not be burned up; it will not consume you." I think about that Scripture and realize that all day I have been turning my back on God, not trusting Him. He has not forsaken me, as I should not forsake Him. All day I have let my sorrows, worries, and tribulations consume me, when I should be looking and turning to God. He has been right here with me all along. I did not die when I hit the water—I came up and out of those seas. He did not let me drown. He was there with me as I lay on the sand trying to catch my breath. He was there with me as I ran along the beach.

He was there with me in the helicopter. He was there with me in the hospital, as He is here with me now. There is a Scripture verse that has followed me around since I was a child. A pastor had prophesied it once to me at a church camp: "For I know the plans I have for you, declares the Lord, Plans to prosper you and not to harm you, plans to give you hope and a future." Here I am thinking that He harmed me, but if you continue to read it, it goes on to say, "Then you will call on me and come and pray to me, and I will listen to you. You will seek me and find me when you seek me with all your heart. I will be found by you, declares the Lord. And I will restore your fortunes and gather you from all the nations and all the places where I have driven you." My twin sister had texted these words in a text message she sent me shortly after my surgery. I had grown up knowing the first verse of that Scripture and strangely never heard the rest of it, but now that I hear the rest of the words, it makes sense.

He isn't harming me—He's waking me up. He wants me to find Him and lean on Him. Of course, right now where I am in my life, the favorite part of that saying is: "I will restore you." Life isn't much without hope. My hope throughout this recovery will be based on that verse out of Jeremiah; I will read that every day.

As I nod off to sleep, I feel the blanket of God's peace cover me.

\*\*\*\*\*\*\*\*\*\*

The following morning I meditate and pray on the decision to rent the cute two-story home. I feel that God wants me to move forward with the application process, so I fill it out and email it right away to the realtor. Almost immediately I get a response that they will do their background work on the app, but most likely I'll get the house.

Most of the next few days are spent packing things up and throwing stuff out. I didn't have much when I moved in, leaving a lot of things behind in my divorce, but somehow I accumulated a lot the last six years.

I receive the call early on a Thursday morning that we got the house. I am relieved knowing we have a place to move into. I haven't said anything to Cruz about the house, so when I tell him that his bedroom is going to have a loft, he jumps up and down in excitement. It makes me feel a lot better about uprooting him, even if it wasn't my decision.

The night before the big move, I decide to relax a little bit and go over to my friend Saige's house. She and her husband Ford have just moved and are having a house warming party. I haven't seen the new house and think it might be a good idea to get out for a change of scenery. Saige and Ford have been long-time friends; we've known one another since our boys were little, and we used to be neighbors.

My mom says she'll come with me, as I know she is looking forward to talking and socializing with people other than me. When we arrive, there are all the same people I'd have expected—her family and her husband's family—but there are a few unexpected surprises. She has a couple friends there whom I've met before and her husband's sister, Tami. I was hesitant to go to this party if there were going to be a lot of people, worried about being bumped into or tripping.

"Oooooh myyyy gosh! I heard what happened, but now that I see you—in this thing—I feel for you!" I look up to see Tami come at me with wide open arms. She is a beautiful, tall blonde with long hair and an amazing personality; she lights up the room wherever she goes. I have known her for five years now; she lives in San Francisco but visits on holidays, which is how I got to know her. I would be stuck home for the holidays, so Saige would always invite me to join their family. We've always had a great time when we see each other; it's just a bummer that she lives so far away.

"Hi! So you heard?" I give her a gentle hug back.

"Yeah, Saige told me. Wow, how long ago did it happen?"

"Two months ago."

"Wow, you look good considering." She smiles and directs me to sit down on the couch.

We sit and catch up. I haven't talked to her since six months prior when she was going through some problems with her boyfriend. She tells me that she broke up with him and just moved back to Huntington

Beach. We reminisce over old times and promise to stay in touch. She offers to help me unpack at the new house, but I politely decline, telling her we should go enjoy our new lives as soon as I'm settled into the new house.

That night, as I lie in my bed for the very last time in this house, I think to myself, *life is really beginning to change*. Six years ago, I moved in here not knowing where I was going or what I was going to do with my life—no job and no friends. Here I am six years later, about to venture into a whole new life. I have a healthy business, healthy son, new friends, and now a second chance at life. *Thank you, God.*

The morning of the move is chaotic. I have my mom take London over to the new house first so that the movers can come in and out freely. Just as I am waiting for the moving van to arrive, a U-Haul pulls up. It's Doug and my missions team.

"Hi, Anne!" he yells out the window. "We wanted to come help you guys out today!"

I cannot believe my eyes. In fact, I start to cry. "Seriously?" This will help me so much; I won't have to pay the movers so much money. They all jump out and start loading up the truck. Just as they leave to the house, the movers show up. The next few hours are busy.

Everything ends up getting moved over to the new house and in one piece. I had been worried about making many, many trips, but they all stepped up and helped me out.  I am realizing how blessed I am.

Once everything is in the house, my mom asks Doug and the team to help pray over the house. We go room to room praying for protection, peace, and blessings. As we go into each room, I feel the presence of God. I know in that moment that this will be a good house.

That evening my mom and I sit on the couch in my new living room, exhausted. She turns and looks at me. "How are you feeling?"

"Not too bad. My back is a little sore. I had to take an Oxycontin before it was time, but it's not as bad as I thought it would be." I've recently downgraded my morphine and Fentanyl to taking Oxycontin every four hours instead. The doctor told me that wearing the Fentanyl patch in the sun is dangerous because it releases the drug when my body temperature increases. I wanted to start tanning again or at least sitting in the sun, so my mom told me I needed to get off of it before she'd let me in the sun again. It's funny, though, because when I heard about the dangerous sun and Fentanyl reaction, I thought of the time I had sat in the sun with Carrie. No wonder I had felt so good that day!

"I talked to Olivia today. She's going to need me to come home at the end of this week or early next week."

"Really? What happened?"

Secretly I am happy because I've been wanting my space, but on the other hand, I'm scared to think of being without her. She's done everything for me: cook, clean, launder the clothes—everything.

"Some people quit and we need to buy some new equipment—just normal things we've been putting off since your accident."

"Oh, yeah. Makes sense; you've been here for a while."

"Anne, I'm worried, though. You're still on some heavy pain killers; they're narcotics. I'm worried about you driving on them."

"Mom, don't worry. I have no reason to drive right now; and now that Tami is living here again, I can ask her for rides."

"Ok, I just don't want anything to happen to you after all that we've been through. I love you, Anne," she starts to cry, "and I don't know if you knew, but this has been extremely hard on me. Taking care of you has brought back a lot of memories of your dad when he broke his back."

My dad had broken his back along with almost every bone in his body when I was fifteen years old. He had fallen several stories onto cement while changing a light bulb in our barn. His recovery was very long, lasting my entire sophomore and junior years in high school. My grandparents on my mom's side had come out for the summer to help my mom.

"I'm sorry, Mom. I will be careful. Trust me, I don't want anything to happen to me, either. I know all of you have gone through enough. I just thank God you were able to take care of me. You know that, right?" I scoot closer to my mom and give her a hug.

We hold on to each other and cry for a few minutes. "Anne, I know God had His hands on you the moment you broke your back. He is going to use this to bring you closer to Him."

"Mom, I know. He already has." I smile.

That night I lie in my new bedroom and thank God. *Thank You for providing this house for me; thank You for making this happen.*

# new beginnings

I wake up to the sun shining directly in my eyes. I roll over. I'm going to have to get some drapes or something for those windows because those blinds don't do any good. I lie there for several minutes, not wanting to get up. I have so much to do; I don't even know where to start. Just then my phone vibrates. I turn and grab it.

It's a message from Cindy: *Good morning! Hope your move went smoothly. I'd like to come over today to help you unpack.*

I text back, *You rock. I'll be here all day.*

Cindy and her daughter Aria show up around noon. They stay all day unpacking and lining the cupboards. They are such a Godsend. I can tell that Aria is getting bored, but Cindy makes her push through it. I feel bad — but they probably feel worse for me.

Over the next several days, my friends show up and just start helping. It's like a dream come true. I'm not the type of person to ask for help, thinking I can do it on my own — and what's great is that my friends know that. So they just show up. Sometimes just showing up does more than anything else you can ever do for someone.

Saige and the kids come by to help organize my closets. Viviane comes by to help hang pictures. Little bits of help here and there add up to a brand new home.

The morning my mom has to leave back home is tough. Although we are both tired of each other by this point, we both knew we'll miss having each other around. My mom will be going back to her empty house, and I'll be here in my empty house all alone with nobody to help me. It's a somber morning, both of us bustling about the house, busy with last-minute things to do.

The drive to the airport is sad, as we chat about the beginning of this journey and how far I have come. She tells me she'll try to make it back down soon and that she'll be praying for me every day. We pull up to the airport and I give her a big hug good-bye. I don't know how to thank her for all she has done. From the moment I called from Bali up to now, she has sacrificed herself for me.

I get into the car. *God, please protect her and watch over her. Please comfort her in peace when she gets home.*

The drive home is lonely; in fact, it's the second time I've driven. My mom had me practice once before, just to make sure I could drive in the cast. The doctor had suggested that I wear it, if possible, in the car, just in case I get into an accident.

I open the door to the house and step in. It's very quiet. I look around. *I can't believe I'm living here. It doesn't seem like home. I miss my home.*

I sit down on the couch and start to cry. *God, please help me get through this. Please help me learn to be alone again.* I am going to have a couple days alone before Cruz comes back from his dad's, so this is going to be a big test for me.

It's a quiet morning and I'm shuffling around the house. I open a box that hasn't been opened yet and look in. Staring right at me is my journal, the one I wrote in during my trip to Indonesia. The pain and hurt come rushing into my heart, and my eyes start to water. I grab it and walk it quickly to my closet and set it down on a stack of other things I need to look through during some down time. As I turn around I hear a voice in my head saying, "It's not the broken back that changed your life. It's Me." I stop and realize that God is trying to tell me something.

"As much as it hurts, Anne, you have to accept My plan for you. Once you accept that this is My entire plan and it's nothing you did wrong, then things will be much easier for you. I have life here on earth filled with things you couldn't even imagine; please learn to fully trust Me and stop blaming everything around you for what has happened. I have great things planned for you, but you wouldn't listen to Me. You struggled with so many things that held you back. I had to push you off that ledge, not to harm you but to bring you closer to Me. Accept what has happened to you and grasp onto the future I have in store for you. It will be beyond your wildest dreams."

At this point I sit down on the edge of my bed and start to bawl, not because of the loss I have experienced but because I realize what an idiot I had been before my accident. I was oblivious to God's plan. I was praying every night and going to church, but I never took the time to really listen to what He was saying. I remember His telling me He had great things in store for me, and I remember that He told me I should end my relationship with Dave—but I didn't act on it. What is really crazy is that I remember asking God to help me change my life in response to His plan and—guess what?— He did. Looking back, He tried in so many ways: my dad's death, the loss of a huge client, the drugging incident, and now my back. I was too stubborn to see His hands reaching out to me, asking me to lean into Him. There's that saying that sometimes God has to tap you on your shoulder or smack you upside the head. Well, for me—he had to break my back.

The rest of my day is spent in a totally different light; I feel that God has given me a gift—a gift of understanding and peace. I decide to call Tami to see if she wants to do something later today.

"Hello there," she answers after the first ring.

"Hi! Would you be up for doing something today?"

"Well, sure—what are you thinking?"

"Honestly, I have no idea; I haven't been out in several months." I really have no idea what I want to do.

"Let me check with my brother. I think Saige's brother is playing at a fundraising event tonight for the Surf Rider Foundation; would you want to go to that?"

"Sure, sounds good to me."

Not too much longer, Tami calls back to say she'll pick me up at seven.

It's my first time out of the house in months; I'm excited and nervous. The thought of someone bumping into me is frightening, but I can't live my life afraid. I dress in jeans and a cute pink tank top; I make sure it is something that will still look cute with the brace. I don't plan on wearing it, but if I start to feel pain, I'll have to put it on.

Tami picks me up at seven exactly. We head down to the hotel hosting the foundation party and valet park. Just before getting out of the car, I ask Tami, "Should I wear my brace?"

"Nah, you'll be ok. We can come back for it if you start hurting."

I leave it in the car and head up to the party with her. What a fun evening—art, music, and dancing . . . At one point I watch a man in a wheelchair on the dance floor spin around to the rhythm of the music. It makes me realize how blessed I am to be standing there watching him.

**********

I've got one last room to unpack and it seems to haunt me every time I sit down to relax. My office is full of boxes, and the only thing set up is my printer—but that doesn't do me any good. I need the office cleaned up so that I can focus on my business. I walk into my office, the hardwood cold under my feet; it's as if every part of my body is dreading this moment. My heart starts to race and I feel faint. I sit down in my new office chair, but it doesn't seem to help. I feel worn out. I've never felt so worn out in my life as I have since my accident. The simplest things exhaust me, and the thought of doing anything makes me panic. *God, why? Why do I have to go through all of this?* My breathing gets heavy and I feel pressure on my chest. *I hate this feeling, God.* My whole life is turned upside down and now I have to figure out how to put it back together. I know asking why isn't going to change anything, but for some reason it's the only thing I can think while tears flow down my cheeks.

I slow down my breathing to catch my breath, it doesn't seem to help. I know I need to get this room unpacked. I lean over and pull the tape off of one box and open it up. God must have been listening, because there's a book inside titled *Your Daily Devotionals.* I'm about to put it to the side when I realize it might be a sign. I turn to today's date and it reads: "Comfort is not given to us when we are lighthearted and cheerful." *Wow, God—You are listening, because that's a fact!* It goes on, "We must travel the depths of emotion in order to experience comfort, one of God's most precious gifts." Then it goes on to say that we go through sorrows and trials in order to feel His grace.

This brings me to a time forty-eight hours after my dad killed himself; a pastor who met with my family quoted Psalm 23:4: "Even though I walk through the valley of the shadow of death, I fear no evil; for You are with me. Your rod and Your staff, they comfort me." He went on to tell us that we *walk through the valley*—we are not supposed to camp out, and we are definitely not supposed to linger. I need to keep walking and not look back. I put the book down and I pray: *God, please give me strength to get through today; it's been hard on me. I need extra strength and especially peace. Amen.*

I spend the rest of the day organizing and preparing my office for actual work. I have been slowly expanding my time taking my meds from four to six hours, when I feel that I can handle it. That night just before bed, as I'm setting my alarm for my next med, I decide to skip an entire four hours, meaning it will be eight hours before I take my next dose of Oxycontin. This way, I'll be able to sleep a solid seven to eight hours.

**********

The following morning I wake up and look at my phone: it's nine a.m. I've been sleeping for nine hours. *Wow—that felt great.* I then remember that I need to take my Oxycontin. I reach over to grab my prescription and hold it in front of me. *Hmm . . . I don't feel any pain.* I decide to wait to see how long I can go without it.

I get out of bed and start my day. It's six hours later that I finally take one, so I decide to wait until I start feeling pain again to take another. *Wow, this is great*, I think to myself. I am definitely not addicted to this stuff. Another day goes by, and I decide to take Advil instead. I say a little prayer thanking God for my recovery and how easy it is to get off of my meds. A lot of people had been worried that I'd get addicted to them, and even though I don't have an addictive personality, they still worry.

As I get ready for bed, I notice that the house is really cold. I've been getting to know the home and noticing that it is falling apart, with cabinet doors breaking and cracks in the wood floors, all things that lead me to believe it is poorly constructed. I decide to put on sweats and a long-sleeved t-shirt. It seems weird in the middle of summer but decide to do it anyway.

I wake up in the middle of the night, freezing. I can't seem to get warm, especially over the last couple days. I wonder if it's all the drugs I've been on breaking down my regulators; this must be how cancer patients feel. I always see them in coats, scarves, and hats; now I understand why. The body must be so tired of fighting the infection, or in my case, my body is trying to heal. The body is so busy fighting the battle that it doesn't have energy to keep warm.

I'm tired of always feeling cold. I'm tired of stepping outside and realizing that everyone is in shorts, tank tops, and flip flops. I am so jealous. I miss that, but the thought of stepping outside in anything except sweats, a heavy sweatshirt, and a beanie chills me to my bones. I'm lying in bed in sweats, tank top, long-sleeved t-shirt, and socks, yet I'm still cold. I reach over and pull my blue fleece blanket around my body under the sheets. *Damn, I'm still cold. Hmm, what else can I do?* I jump out of bed and go to my closet, standing there looking at my clothes. It dawns on me: a beanie! I grab a black beanie from my hat collection and put it on. After crawling back into bed, I realize that's what hits the spot—and I nod off to sleep.

**********

Today is a big day. I am going to meet with the pastors at the church and discuss what has happened to me. I haven't heard from the senior pastor since waiting for my helicopter on the island. I expected a visit at the hospital or at least a phone call. I was already disappointed with how they handled my transportation off that island, and now this has made it worse. It's as if they're trying to ignore the fact that I broke my back while working for them. I had reached out to them a few days ago, requesting to speak to both the senior pastor and the pastor replacing him. The current senior pastor, Pastor Barlow, is retiring in a couple months, so part of me thinks that maybe things slipped through with the transferring of titles. Pastor Sean is the new pastor coming in. The other part of me wonders if he even knew what happened to me. So the point in meeting with them today is to make sure they both know the entire story and to see what they are doing with their missions work moving forward, to prevent a break in communication, as in my case.

Although I am off of my prescription pain killers, I ask Tami to drive with me to the church and sit in on the conversation. I want someone to be there supporting me and also as a witness to what they say.

As I get ready for the meeting, I look in the mirror. My body has completely deteriorated: my legs are skinny and pale, my arms thin as rails, and my face gaunt. I strap on my brace and say a prayer. *God, please give me the right words to say and give them open hearts.*

Tami picks me up right on time, leaving us a couple minutes to get to the church, which is just around the corner. We pull into the parking lot, just steps from the office. Tami and I get out and walk upstairs. Things seem a bit familiar, but I can't put my finger on it. We exit the elevator and see a receptionist sitting in front of us. She smiles. "Can I help you?"

"Yeah, we're here to see Pastor Barlow and Pastor Sean. I think Mark will be here, too," I respond with a confident tone. We are the only ones here in the church office. Who else are they expecting to walk up in a body cast? I step off to the side and see Mark make his way over to us. Mark is the pastor's assistant; I called him to schedule the meeting.

"Hi," I say with a hug. "This is my friend Tami."

"Yes. How are you?" He shakes her hand. Just then Pastor Sean walks towards us.

"Hi, Pastor Sean. I'm Anne Latour. I don't think we have officially met," I say with a smile, shaking his hand. Pastor Sean is a young man coming over from youth ministries.

"I'm Sean. Nice to formally meet you, Anne," he says, shaking my hand. I am not the greatest at reading people, but I can see that he seems to be a real person, a genuine guy. His eyes seem sincere and his hand shake is firm, but not too firm; that tells a lot about a person. "Come this way. I apologize if it's too cold, but the conference room is the only room we have that will fit all of us."

"It's all good," I say as we walk towards the back of the building. Pastor Sean opens the door to a room and we walk in. I'm feeling a sense of familiarity as we walk in. This is the room my team first met in, the day I decided to join the trip. A wave of emotion overwhelms me as I look around at the long mahogany table and black leather chairs, the windows along the back wall—it's all the same.

"Wow, this is where it all began." I sit down at the table across from Pastor Sean and Mark. My eyes glance around the room again quickly, as not to tear up, but I can't help it.

"This is where it all began . . ." I say again, trying to hold back the tears. I look at Sean and then at Mike and try not to look at Tami. This is hard to say to strangers, let alone to a friend. It's not easy pouring out your heart. "I had never planned on going on that missions trip; God led me there—led me here." I go on to explain how God called me to be there, to be where I was, and to ultimately be with me when I broke my back.

The meeting goes as I expect. I explain where I'm coming from and what I expected from the church. I also explain what my concerns are moving forward with the church. It seems as if Pastor Sean and Mark are on board with me and understand where I am coming from.

Near the end of the meeting, Pastor Barlow shows up and the mood shifts. He makes everything out to be a joke; he starts off with laughter and continues with a non-serious attitude.

This is my life. This is what I have for my future. There is absolutely nothing funny about it. Pastor Barlow has taken this lightly from the beginning, and here, as I am sitting in his conference room, he's doing it again. I don't want to make a big deal of it as I'm sitting here; I just had a great meeting with the others—until Pastor Barlow walked in. I will not let it affect my attitude on the church or this new pastor.

We end the meeting with not much more said; Pastor Barlow has ruined it all. We say our good-byes and walk downstairs.

As Tami and I get into her car, she looks over at me and asks, "Did he really just say that?"

"You mean when I said I'd really like to go back to Indonesia, and Pastor Barlow responded, 'not on our dime'?"

"YES!"

"Yeah, he did—and now that I think about it, I wish I had asked him if he knew that I had raised most of the money for the entire group."

I sat there in the car looking at Tami, feeling hurt and somewhat abandoned. Pastor Barlow was someone I had looked up to. I had always looked forward to going to church just to see and hear him speak; and right now, I am disgusted by his behavior. How could such a godly person act in such a selfish and uncompassionate way?

"I am never coming back to this church again," Tami says, starting her car. "That was rude."

"Yeah, but we have to give the new pastor a chance."

I know Tami just started going back to church and reaching back to God; I would hate for something like this to affect her spiritual journey.

"Let's go somewhere," she says with a chipper voice.

"Okay, where?" I know she's trying to cheer me up, knowing I'm bummed from the meeting.

"Let's go to Laguna! I haven't been there in ages."

She backs her car up and we drive to Laguna Beach. It's a beautiful day, and everyone's out on the beach and shopping in the stores—a typical summer day. I haven't been out in a while, except to go to the doctor's office and Saige's that one night. It seems like I'm seeing everything for the first time, even though it's only been a few months. Some things have changed.

We pull up to a fairly popular restaurant, known for its outside seating overlooking the ocean.

"This is going to be fun," Tami says, getting out of the car and handing her key to the valet.

I decide to leave my brace in the car, as I'll get too much unwanted attention if I wear it inside.

We walk in and see a table along the windows set for two. "Is that table available?" I ask the hostess.

"Yes—first come, first served."

We sit down and order a glass of Chardonnay right away. I haven't had any wine since Saige's housewarming party, so this should be good, especially now that I'm off my meds.

As we sit and reminisce about the last year, a very handsome man approaches our table.

"Excuse me, ladies, but can my friends and I join you? The hostess said that your table can seat four people and—see over there." He points to a table behind us, which is smaller than ours. "We have a table that only seats two, but there are four of us."

Tami and I look at each other with the "he's hot" look, and she replies with a smile, "Only if you buy us a drink."

"Of course. What do you want?"

"Two Chardonnays!" She smiles flirtatiously.

He walks away, saying something to the other guys. They are all very good looking with dark hair and dark complexions, and wearing business-like attire.

Tami looks at me. "He's hot."

"Yeah, I've been watching them. They're all really cute."

He comes back over and introduces himself and his friend.

"Hello ladies. This is Mirza, and I am Shemar."

We have a nice time chatting and getting to know them. They are both doctors, Mirza a pediatrician and Shemar a radiologist. Shemar tells me he is a Christian and is active in his church; he also has a son, who is close to Cruz's age. Just before leaving, Shemar asks for my phone number. I haven't been on a date in months, and think it might be nice to get out and let a man spoil me.

After we get in the car, Tami looks at me. "So?"

"So what?" I smile, knowing what she's asking. She had seen Shemar get my phone number.

"You know!"

"Yes, I gave him my phone number; he's really nice. He met his ex-wife at church."

"Oh MY God! Does that make him a Christian?" she says, laughing.

I laugh, too. "Not really, I guess—but he's a doctor—and he's really cute!"

"It's worth a date! And you deserve to have fun. Let loose!"

We drive home chatting about the guys we had just met and that it would be funny if, after all this time, I end up meeting and marrying a doctor.

\*\*\*\*\*\*\*\*\*\*

The next morning I wake up to a text from Shemar: *Good morning, Anne.*
*Hi, Shemar!*
*When can I take you to dinner?*
*I'm available tomorrow night and Tuesday night.*
*I'm working late Monday. Let's do Tuesday.*
*Perfect.*
*Ok, shoot me your address and I'll pick you up at seven o'clock on Tuesday.*

I put my phone down and smile. *God, is this the one?* I sit to do my devotions for most of the morning and then get ready for the day. Today I tell Carrie that I'll hang out with her at my old neighborhood pool. I haven't been back there since I moved and I know it'll be weird, but I haven't seen her in a long time and I know she spends her weekends at the pool. Today is the only day to go over because I get Cruz back tomorrow.

I pack up a bag and drive over to the old hood. My clicker still works, so I enter through the gates without a problem. As I pull in, I look around. This seems weird, being here as a visitor. I park my car and walk up to the pool in my turtle shell brace, and with my bag, again feeling like a stranger in my own neighborhood—well, in my *old* neighborhood.

Carrie welcomes me with a Bloody Mary, our typical pool libation. Her son is lying out in the sun next to her with an empty chair on the opposite side. He's a good-looking young man, in his mid-twenties.

"Hi, Brian!" I say, setting up my lounge chair, draping a white towel over the back. "How are you?"

"Could be better—I just broke up with my fiancée."

"Aww, I am so sorry!"

Carrie had already filled me in, but I pretend to be surprised. Brian is a good guy and deserves better anyway; they're better off apart.

It's nice hanging out and catching up. I tell them I'm going to start physical therapy next week and that I recently went cold turkey on my meds.

"Wow, Anne, I am so proud of you!" Carrie toasts the good news. "You were on some heavy stuff, girl. I was worried."

"Thanks!"

Brian holds up his glass. "You didn't have any withdrawals?"

"Nope, none!" We toast.

"Usually people will have the shakes or night sweats. I had woken up freezing. Most people overheat, but I was freezing—and my stomach was a mess!"

I just now realize with surprise that I was having withdrawals all that time that I was freezing. It wasn't the house being poorly insulated; I was going through withdrawal. Plus I had stomach problems, but I thought it was because I had eaten gluten.

"I did have withdrawals after all!" Carrie and Brian look at me. "I was freezing, I couldn't get warm. I'd take hot showers and still couldn't get warm enough. All this time I thought my new house was poorly insulated! Oh my gosh!"

We all start laughing and Carrie raises her glass for another toast. "Thank God you didn't know it was withdrawals, otherwise it might have been harder for you to get off of them."

We toast and continue laughing. What a moment of enlightenment. All that time I thought I was special and had zero complications coming off my narcotics…

The following morning, I wake up early to pick Cruz up from his dad's. Normally I wouldn't get him until Wednesday, but his dad has a meeting today, so he asked me to get him early.

I pull up to Jeff's house and Cruz runs out. "Mom, are we going to church?"

"Um, sure. I was thinking we could go to breakfast, but if you want to go to church instead, we can."

"Yeah, church instead."

He smiles, so I head to church reluctantly. I've wanted to find a new church, but I haven't taken the time to research any. The church I really want to go to is Saddleback, but it's too far of a drive—plus today is the first day the new pastor will be preaching, so it'll be interesting to see if there are any changes.

As we walk downstairs to the café area, I can hear that the pastor has already started talking. We take our seats at a table by ourselves and sit back to hear the sermon. The pastor's sermon today is about how we as Christians should become a bigger movement within our church and partake in church activities and small groups. He goes on to say that the church is here for us; they are here to serve us as we are to serve them. It made me question the church and how they reacted to my accident. If I am here to serve the church and that's what the church is about, then how does the church make sure they are here for me—especially when something goes wrong while I am serving with them? Why did I have to reach out to the church to help me when I needed help? Why didn't they come to me and ask if I needed anything?

Tears fill my eyes while the pastor is praying about how the church is here for us. I feel hurt within my heart, but most of all anger. I don't want to feel anger towards them; I like it here, and I know Cruz likes it here. How do I overcome this hurt and pain? Where was the church when I was hurt? Why is it that he preaches that the church is here for me when they weren't? It couldn't have been clearer for them. I broke my back while serving God in their church.

I pray, trying to hold back the tears. *God, I pray to you right now to help me overcome this anger, this hurt, and this pain. I don't want this to affect me on a level I'll never be able to come back from.*

What the pastor said sticks with me. I have to take moments to myself throughout the day to meditate on peaceful thoughts. I am broken physically and mentally, feeling exhaustion on many levels. I know that with God's help, I can overcome my hurt and anger, but it will take work— a lot of work.

# three month post op

The following day I drop Cruz back off at his dad's and head back home to sleep. I've been extremely tired lately, and doing little things becomes strenuous and exhausting. I have my date with Kevin the following night, so I rest all day.

Tuesday evening rolls around quickly. I've already texted Kevin my address and am patiently waiting for him to pick me up. We are going to dinner downtown. It's a laid-back surfer town, so I decide to wear jeans and a teal blouse, which brings out the green in my eyes. I've decided not to wear my brace, as he doesn't know much about my story yet.

He pulls up a little after seven o'clock, a little late, but I'll let it pass this one time. He comes to my door, and like a gentleman walks me to his car. We drive the short distance to a sushi restaurant downtown and get seated right away. The evening goes well, starting with small talk about sports, and then we get into politics. The subject seems to get under his skin, so he excuses himself to go to the bathroom. I'm thinking that he wants to change the subject and doesn't know how.

When he arrives back to the table, he smells of cigarettes.

"Do you smoke?" I ask, looking at him, smelling the air.

He looks away and then laughs. "Yeah, but only when I drink." He holds up his glass of wine and raises his eyebrows.

*Hmmm . . . At least it's just when he drinks.* The night continues and we end up back at my house. I've already had a couple glasses of wine, so my inhibitions are down. I invite him in.

We open a bottle of wine and go outside. It's a warm night, so I light my fire pit. We cuddle up on the patio furniture and I tell him my story. He is intrigued and tells me that in his professional opinion, I have recovered very fast.

"Can I see the scar?"

"Sure." I tend to show everyone my scars, as they represent a new me, something I'm proud of. I turn my back to him and slowly pull up the back of my blouse; he reaches over and helps me hold it up.

"Wow." he traces the scar with his fingers. "The doctor did a really good job."

"Really?" I have no idea what a spinal surgery scar is supposed to look like, so I'll take his word for it. Besides, he's a doctor.

All of a sudden I feel his breath on my back and then his lips. He's kissing my back. *Damn, this feels weird.* Since coming home from the hospital, I've always wondered what it would be like with a man after my surgery—if a man would even touch my back. He continues to kiss my back and slowly pulls my blouse up over my head. His kisses lead to my neck and then he slowly turns me around to him. I kiss him back passionately. Things continue to get heated, and he carries me into my living room and lays me on my couch, taking off my jeans. I am now wearing only my bra and underwear. While kissing me, he takes off his shirt, showing his toned, hard abs in the moonlight coming through the windows. I start to kiss his chest.

I stop and sit up. "Um, no—this can't happen."

"What?" he stops kissing me and sits back. "Are you serious?"

"Yeah, you need to leave."

"Wooooaaah, slow down. What's going on? Did I hurt you?"

"No, you didn't. Sorry, but I haven't had sex in three months, and I'm not sure if I even can." I grab a blanket on the edge of the couch and wrap myself in it, covering my body.

"Oh, okay. When do you go to the doctor again?"

"This week, actually."

"So, once he clears you, we'll make love right here and over there," he points to the stairs, "and over there . . ." He keeps pointing around the house.

"Well, actually, I had promised myself before I broke my back, that I wouldn't have sex with anyone until I was in a committed relationship, or maybe even marriage."

He looks at me and laughs. "Are you effing kidding me? Marriage?"

"Yeah, I'm not really sure. I've gone three months without sex; maybe I can hold off completely."

"Well, I understand the relationship idea, but not until marriage—what kind of guy would wait that long?" He laughs and taps me on my leg.

"I don't know. Yeah, seems silly," I laugh.

We sit there a while longer, cooling off and talking about our past relationships. It feels really good just talking with him, even though I want to do many other things. He kisses me good-bye and says he'll call tomorrow.

I go to sleep that night feeling really good about myself, saying a prayer of thanks for helping me stay strong, even though I had been tempted by a hot doctor. It seems like Kevin respected my wish not to have sex and is interested in pursuing a relationship.

**********

I'm awake but I don't want to open my eyes. I know that as soon as my eyes open, they will signal the brain that I'm up, and I don't want to think right now. I have too much on my mind and I refuse to wake up. I toss and turn. *Damn.* I can't stay in bed. I slowly push myself up, being careful not to exacerbate any pain. Rubbing the sleep from my eyes, I look at my phone. It's seven o'clock and he still hasn't responded. Kevin and I have been texting each other the last couple of days, but when I asked him when he had another free night, he just went silent on me. I guess he's over me. *God, please give me the peace and the self-control today not to contact him.* I feel that God is again telling me that this guy is not right for me and I need to move forward. Why is it so hard to do that? The only thing this guy has going for him is that he is good looking and he's a doctor! He smokes, drinks way too much, and doesn't even have custody of his son. *Anne, wake up!* He's a loser; there are red flags going up everywhere.

Now that my brain is turning, I get out of bed and make my way downstairs to make coffee. London is waiting by the door. "Good morning, girl." I open the door and she happily runs out. I think to myself, *why can't I be that care free?*

I have a big day ahead. The doctor's appointment will determine whether I can start being active again and if I can stop wearing my turtle shell. Although I've been slacking on wearing it, I feel fairly good about this appointment today. I can't believe it's been three months since my accident; it seems much longer. There's no way I'd have thought I'd be this far along. When I was laid up in my hospital, it seemed as if time had stood still. Staying in the present kept me sane, and that's what I needed at the time. I make myself some coffee and head upstairs. I have some work-related emails to get out before I can leave for my doctor's appointment.

As I drive down towards my doctor's office, emotions start to roll in. I'm seeing familiar sights as I exit the freeway; things I saw back when I was holding a puke bucket and having thoughts of despair. Although I'm doing much better, I can't help but think back to those first few weeks. My eyes start to water as I come to an intersection in front of the hospital. I am supposed to go left, but something tells me to go straight. I pull forward through the intersection and I see it: the old white and weathered sign that reads AMBULANCE in red staring down at me. I turn down the street and see the ambulance entrance to the hospital. Memories start pouring in: the bumpy ride from LAX, my mom and friend waiting, the surgery. Tears are flowing down my face. *God, I know there is a reason for all of this; please give me the faith to embrace my new life.* I drive quickly around the emergency entrance and back onto the street. It's tough seeing the hospital, but I think it is a good step in the right direction for my recovery, as I need to confront my fears.

I pull into the parking lot and immediately get a front row parking spot. Good start. The waiting room is packed as usual, so I find my seat in the corner. After waiting what seems like forever, I get called back. The girls at the orthopedic group are super nice; they take me through all the x-rays and put me in a waiting room. I'm a little nervous, but I feel at peace. My doctor comes in looking rather good, dressed in a sleek blue suit and striped shirt.

"Hello, Anne," the doctor says as he sits down on the stool. "Your films look great. Are you ready to be done with your brace?"

"Oh my gosh, yes! Really? I've been looking forward to this day." I am overwhelmed with relief and excitement. "Does that mean I can start physical therapy?"

"You've been healing great, Anne. Look here." He's pointing at the x-ray. The titanium brackets are now surrounded by white lines. When I looked at the x-rays six weeks ago, there was empty black space.

"Is that all bone?" I point to the white marks surrounding the nuts and bolts.

He nods. "Yes, it's growing into the cage. In three more months it'll all be white."

I sit back and smile. What a relief. Although I knew I hadn't done any damage, I had been a little bit concerned that there might be a setback.

"So, I know this is a crazy question, but is there anything I can't do once I'm healed?"

He leans back and chuckles. "You can do anything you want—just don't jump off cliffs anymore! But in all seriousness, don't run or do any jumping for at least six more weeks. You are still healing, and the less impact you put on your back the better. The bone will be completely healed in three more months. At that point, there's not much damage you can do."

"Awesome! You have no idea how worried I was. I feel so much better."

"You'll be fine, Anne." He hands me the script for physical therapy and walks out of the room.

I look at my turtle shell brace and smile. I know this isn't over; it's really just the beginning of another phase in my life—but it's a good one. Working out is my favorite thing, and physical therapy will be a breeze.

I am in a much better mood as I drive home. I need to let everyone know, so of course I start with Mom.

"Hello?" she answers.

"Mom, great news—I get to take off my brace!"

"Wonderful! Did the doctor say how much physical therapy you need?"

I look down at the prescription. "It says one to two times a week for six weeks."

"That's great, Anne. Do you know where you'll go?"

"I'm not sure yet; I need to look into a couple places." Dave had told me about some places that specialize in professional athletes. I should look into those first because they will know how to work with me, since I am very active in my daily life.

"Ok. Keep me posted." I can sense her hesitation.

"Mom? You okay?"

"Yes, I just thank God you are okay," she says with a heavy breath. "I was worried that you might have done something during the move."

"Yeah—me, too, Mom. Ok, I gotta' make some calls," I say, trying to end the conversation. "Love you, Mom."

"Love you, too. Bye."

I say a quiet prayer. *Thank You for protecting me, God; thank You for continuing to heal me.*

I make a couple more phone calls, one to my older sister Olivia, and I leave a message for my twin sister before calling Dave.

"Hello, Miss," Dave answers. I'm not sure why I'm calling him; it's been six weeks since I've seen him. We've talked on the phone a couple times, but I have a feeling he's seeing someone. It's weird, but I feel as if Kevin helped me get over Dave; as much as I don't want to resurrect old feelings, I would like to share the good news with him. After all, he was a big part of my recovery, and he is one of my closest friends.

"Hey there. I have great news. I just got out of my doctor's office," I pause for the dramatic finish. "I don't have to wear my brace anymore! Doc says I am healing and I can start PT now."

"Great news, Miss!" he says. "You're a power healer. I expected nothing less."

"Thanks." I'm blushing.

"Let's celebrate with dinner tonight?" he says.

"Ummm . . ." I'm not sure if I'm ready to see him yet. I feel like I'm over him, and if I see him, the emotions might come rushing back.

"If not tonight, it'll be a while before I can see you again," he quickly says, as if he knows I'm hesitating. "I have class and some business trips."

"Ok, I'll move some things around," I lie as if I have a busy schedule, when all I have is a warm bath and maybe dinner in front of the TV.

"Cool. I'll see you at seven-thirty."

"I'll text you my new address," I say, hanging up. He hasn't seen my new place and I had wanted to keep it that way. I have zero memories of him here, which is really nice—much easier for me to move on with my new life.

**********

I am wearing my white shorts which show off my now skinny legs. I decide to go simple as he's always wearing basketball shorts and a t-shirt. I have a cute purple tank on but will probably have to change into a sweat shirt because the air conditioning is usually blasting in restaurants this time of year.

My phone rings. "Hello?" It's Cruz and he has his first day of school tomorrow. He's probably nervous and needs some loving words.

"Hi, Mom. Are you going to be at my classroom before school starts?" he asks with a whisper. He must be sneaking the phone call; he whispers when his dad doesn't want him talking to me.

"Of course, bud! I wouldn't miss it!" I respond with a chipper voice. "Are you nervous?"

"Yeah, kinda', Mom."

"Don't be nervous. You are going to love it—and you get to see all of your old friends."

"Ok, Mom. I gotta' go."

"Love you, bud. See you tomorrow."

"Love you, too, Mom." He is such a sweet kid. I'm happy he found time to call me. I'll have to remember to wake up early for the first day of school. I set my alarm twice thirty minutes apart to be sure and not snooze through it. Just as I finish, I hear the doorbell. As I walk to the front door I quietly say a prayer: *God, please give me the strength and the peace to get through this night without having sex.*

"Hey, there," I say, giving him a hug. He steps in and smiles.

"Good to see you out of the shell. You look amazing."

I blush. "Thanks, Dave. It feels great to be done with that thing."

I show him around the house. I still have some things sitting on the floor, pictures and art work that still need to be hung up. It's weird, though—I'm not embarrassed. Dave is a close friend and I've gotten over caring what he thinks anymore. As we walk around the house looking at each room, I feel nothing toward him. Normally I'd want to hug him, hold his hand, or just be near him, but right now I don't have that feeling.

We eat dinner at a sports bar around the corner from my house. It's somewhat empty and loud with baseball games blaring on the TV screens. We talk about everything, from what he's been doing to what I've been up to. I don't have much to say about myself, as I haven't done anything exciting this summer. He asks if I have anything planned, and I tell him I will probably go back to Indonesia in the spring. As I am sitting there looking at him, I wonder why I was ever so attracted to him. Maybe God answered my prayers and took away his good looks—or maybe his lack of commitment has made him unattractive. Yes—that's it!

When we finish dinner, we head back to my house. On the way he tells me that he has to get home to do laundry because he's leaving early in the morning. As he pulls into my driveway, I tell him that it was nice seeing him.

"Sorry I couldn't stay longer, Miss," he says as he hugs me over the console.

"It's all good; I have some work to finish up." I pull away quickly so he can't kiss me. I turn and get out of the car just as fast. "Thanks again for dinner; have fun in the Bay."

He smiles and I shut the door. *Whew—that was easy.* It's as if we've never dated. I head into the house and let London inside; she's probably ready to go to bed on her comfy doggy pillow. I am tired and I have an early morning ahead of me with Cruz's first day of school, so I head to bed.

Just before lying down, I pray. *Dear God, thank You for giving that amazing strength to see Dave and not be drawn to him like before. I know You work miracles, and I believe You are doing just that, right now, in my life. Thank You. Amen.*

Just as I pull the covers over my shoulders, my phone vibrates. I roll over and grab it thinking that Kevin has finally responded.

It reads: *Sorry I didn't stay longer. Always a pleasure to see you, though, and so happy to hear you are doing better.*

Go figure. He can't just let the night be over; we said our good-byes. I'm frustrated now but want to take this opportunity to let him know that staying longer wasn't going to be an option.

*It's all good. It's better that way. Great seeing you as well. Take care and good luck with school.*

He responds: *Better that way?*

Of course he doesn't get it or he just wants to draw this out. I think to myself for a few minutes. I need to respond with something good, something that says that late nights that turn into "hit it and leave it" will not fly anymore. When is he ever going to get it? I want more than fly-by-night hook-ups. What I really want is a man to sleep with every night, a man who will be by my side for the rest of my life. I thought that could have been him, but he's made it clear he just wants sex with an emotional relationship that he can control on his timing.

*I enjoy your company—don't take that the wrong way. I just think we need to move on. We had a strong physical attraction to each other which didn't help matters. Seeing each other at night typically led to sleepovers and . . . It's been three months; best to keep it that way.* I ended it with a wink. I turned my phone off and pulled the covers back up over me.

**********

I wake up at five o'clock in the morning. *Darn it.* I can't get back to sleep. I push myself up and adjust some pillows behind me. It seems so much easier now that I know I can twist, turn, and bend. What a mental block that brace was. I roll over and turn the light on; the sun is starting to come across my bedroom windows but there isn't enough light to read the small print in the Bible. I spend some time in devotions and then head downstairs for my coffee. After last night's dinner with Dave, I feel rejuvenated and powerful, as if I can conquer anything in my path.

I open the door for London and step outside. What a beautiful day; the sun is already high in the sky and it's very warm. I grab my phone to text Tami; we should definitely do something outside today. I need to celebrate my brace coming off.

Time seems to fly—it's seven-forty already. I pour my coffee into a travel cup and head out the door to Cruz's school. It's his first day of the last year at this school. He's now at the top of his class. I feel emotions build up as I drive to the school.

*Darn it, Anne—you do this every year!* I tell myself. *Don't cry in front of him!*

I pull into the school and find a parking spot in the back. Not bad; it'll be an easy exit. Cruz's school is a fairly new, built only fifteen years ago. I used to live next door to the principal, so I've always thought we got special treatment when it came to placing Cruz with teachers. The last time I saw her, I was at the school play four days after returning from the hospital. I looked like absolute crap: skinny, pale, and in a wheelchair. I want to believe that she went above and beyond this year while placing Cruz in a fifth-grade class . . .

I park the car and start walking to his classroom, seeing a lot of parents and old neighbors along the way. Everyone is commenting on the absence of my brace, and it feels great. I've come a long way from the last time everyone saw me. If they only knew.

Cruz sees me and comes running to me. "Mom!" he yells.

"Hey, bud." I give him a big hug. "Are you nervous?"

"A little bit, but Jack's in my class!"

"That's awesome," I say with a smile. We are standing outside his classroom surrounded by a bunch of kids and parents waiting to be let in. Just as I walk towards a parent I know, the doors open and all the kids start rushing inside. I look over at Cruz.

"Bye, bud. Have fun and remember—the first impression is your last impression." He smiles and turns to walk into his classroom.

As I head back to my car, I see a text message from Tami. *Hey, girl. Let's bike downtown.*

I message her back. *Let's meet at Longboards—noon.*
*Sounds good, girly!*

I've really enjoyed the friendship that has been developing with her. She is a good person with a good heart, and I love that she is a person of faith.

I'm standing at the garage door thinking about canceling, making up some excuse about being called to a client's office. I'm nervous about getting on my bike. I don't know why I'm so scared—but the thought of falling or getting hurt is nerve-racking. I take the first step to conquering my fear and open the door. I step outside. As I walk around the car to my bike, I tell myself that if the tires are low, I'll skip the ride. If the wheels squeak, I'll cancel. If . . . If . . . *Darn it, Anne! Shut up and stop making excuses—you are going to ride your bike today!*

I grab the handles and wheel it around to the outside of the garage. I put it on the stand and look at it. I press down on the tires—good air. I step back again. It looks good. I can't find any reason not to get on it. I flip the kick stand up and slowly swing my leg over the bike and move it forward with a swift push. *Wow, this feels good.* I smile. *This actually feels really good!* I ride up the street, looking like a big kid, I'm sure, grinning from ear to ear as if I've just learned to ride a bike for the first time. I pull back into my driveway and put the bike inside the garage.

*Ring! Ring!* Tami's calling me. "Hey, girl!" I say.

"I am so sorry, but I have to cancel. My mom needs some help packing for her trip." I could hear her disappointment. Her mom is going on a two-week cruise to Alaska and had just broken a rib.

"It's okay, T. We can do it another time. Seriously, no big deal!" It kind of *is* a big deal, but I'm not going to say so. I was looking forward to riding bikes downtown and I finally took the big leap of faith and got on my bike... *Oh well.* At least I rode it. I walk back into the house and shut the garage door.

**\*\*\*\*\*\*\*\*\*\***

It's my first day of physical therapy and I'm excited but a little nervous. It's been three months since my surgery and I haven't done any exercising.

The doctor wanted me to protect my back, so the only thing I've been able to do is walk. The thought of working muscles that are now atrophied scares the life out of me. I had decided to go with the same physical therapist, Marty, whom I had used back when I had knee issues. I had been told by a couple doctors that I would need exploratory knee surgery, but after going to Marty, I was able to avoid surgery.

I see him as soon as I walk in the door; he's standing at the front desk talking to the receptionist. Marty is a short energetic Italian guy with dark curly hair and freckles. He always has a smile on his face and is ready to help anyone who asks. He'd be the guy to give his last buck away to someone in need.

"Anne!" He greets me with a big smile and a hug. "How are you? You look great considering the last time I saw you—you were only two weeks out of the hospital."

"Thanks! I'm feeling good. I feel like God gave me a second chance at life and now a second chance at a new body!"

There are some other physical therapists standing nearby who look over in my direction. They probably aren't used to hearing such positive attitudes here. I've noticed along my path of recovery that people seem to be surprised by my positive outlook.

"Well, that's the spirit, Anne! Follow me. I am going to do an evaluation on you, and then we'll start you with some simple exercises."

The facility seems small, but if this is where Marty is working, then this is where I'll be. One side of the room has a row of therapy tables. On the opposite wall there are a couple weight machines, and on another wall Pilates machines. He helps me up onto one of the tables and starts to ask me questions while checking my mobility.

After the evaluation, he introduces me to his aids who will be helping me. The exercises are small, simple movements, focusing on my core strength, which at this point is nil. My first day of physical therapy lasts two hours, but when I am done, I feel great. I want to call Dave to tell him how excited I am, but I'm not sure where we stand. Things have been lonely without him; he never responded to my last text message, so I assume he got my point and agrees that we should have a strictly platonic friendship. Part of me wonders if I will ever hear from him again. If he knows that the sex is done, then he might be done with us. It's sad to consider, but if this is what God wants, then I will gladly accept it. He doesn't need to break my back again to get a point across. No way—never again.

The next couple of months leading up to the holidays consists of physical therapy and, when time allows, working on growing my business. As the holidays approach, I start getting excited at the thought of seeing my sister Olivia and her husband. I haven't had visitors since I moved in and have felt a bit lonely, wishing more than ever before that I had a man to share my life with. Thanksgiving will be a nice break from my daily routine and I hope to be healthy enough to enjoy some site-seeing and the typical tourist things they like to do while visiting.

Just as I'm about to call her to confirm her flight reservations, my phone rings. I look down at my phone and see it's her.

"Hi!" she says. "How is physical therapy coming along?"

"I love it!"

"It's not hard? Does it hurt?"

"Not really, but I do have days I don't want to go; but then I think about how I could be in a wheelchair and not even have the choice to be doing this type of physical therapy . . ." I sigh. "So no, it's not hard—it could be worse."

"I am so proud of you, Anne. I'm glad you have such a positive attitude about this. I've been praying for you, and I really think God is answering my prayers."

"Thanks, Olivia. As I keep telling people, God gave me a second chance at life. I'm not going to mess this chance up!"

"Do you think you'll be able to go to Universal Studios when we come down? Luke has wanted to take Cruz, and we've never been. Thought it would be fun to do something different."

"I'm sorry, Olivia. I'm not sure if I can go on any rides, and to be honest, I wouldn't take the chance anyway—but please don't hold back on account of me. Cruz loves Universal Studios."

"Are you sure? I'd hate for you to stay home. Maybe you can come and hang out with us anyway."

"Nah, but thank you. Seriously, I'm good with it. I have a lot to do with physical therapy and work. I'll just stay home and work. You guys can take my car."

"Well, we can talk about the logistics when we get there." She then asks, "So, anything else new with you? Dating anyone?"

"No. I wish . . . I've been thinking about doing the online dating thing."

"Really? I thought you weren't going to do that?"

"Yeah, I know, but I think God is telling me to do it."

"Well, if God is telling you, then you should. I've heard of people meeting and getting married through it. Maybe you'll meet someone."

"Yeah, who knows . . . After everything I've been through, my focus isn't on finding a husband anymore; it's more about God and being the best person I can be for my friends and family."

She laughs. "Anne, God always seems to have a different timeline and plan from ours."

"True."

"I'll email you the flight reservations tomorrow. We will get in before Thanksgiving."

"Ok, thank you. I cannot wait to see you."

I put my phone down next to my laptop and turn the TV on. Just then a commercial comes on about a dating website. I wonder if this is a sign. I've seen a lot of commercials recently advertising dating websites, and just yesterday, I overheard a friend of a friend talking about dating men from an online site. I do a quick search of the top Christian dating sites and the one that I keep hearing about pops up. As I register, I say a prayer. *God, if this is what I am supposed to do, I just ask that You direct and guide me through this process, as You will always be my priority.*

Immediately I receive a bunch of matches from men who see my profile. They start the process of getting to know me by sending me messages or asking me questions. I am feeling overwhelmed as I scroll over several pictures and click on a few profiles. My heart is starting to race, and I feel like I want to throw my computer across the room. What the heck did I just do?

I shut my computer down and put my head in my hands. *God, this seems like a lot of work. Please give me patience to get through this.*

I get up and walk downstairs to my kitchen, reaching into the fridge for a bottle of water. I feel God's presence, and all of a sudden I am at peace. Walking back upstairs I feel that God wants me to look at the site again, so I turn the computer on and log on. Taking a deep breath, I start to scroll over the profile pictures of the men who contacted me. There's one—a man named Devon out of Pasadena. He's good looking and close to my age. His page says that he has kids and that he might want more, but most importantly his priority is God. *Hmm, that sounds nice . . .* It's so refreshing to see that there really are men who put God first. I answer his questions and continue the line of communication that the dating website recommends. *This might not be too hard*, I think to myself, as I delete a few unattractive matches. I don't base everything on looks, but they have to at least be decent for me to spend time looking at their profile page.

Just then, I scroll over the photo of a good-looking man who appears to be deep in thought. *Interesting.* I click on the profile and start to read: Blake, fifty-one years old . . . *Ok, a little older than me, but since when has age stopped me?* My ex-husband is fourteen years older and one of my good friends is happily married to a man twenty-seven years her senior. As I read, I become more interested in this man and my heart is in my throat. He is passionate about adventure and involved in foreign missions, as his pictures depict. The most influential person in his life is Jesus. *Wow!* I quickly respond to his questions, but just before I send him my questions, I look over his profile one more time. *Oh no!* He lives in Michigan. How did that happen? I must not have set a limit as to how far away my matches can be. *Yikes.* How would that ever work—Michigan? I've never been in a long-distance relationship, but I certainly have dated my fair share of men who travel for business, so maybe this wouldn't be that bad—if this is what God wants. I say a little prayer just before sending him my list of questions, one of which asks how it could be possible to have a relationship living so far apart.

After sending off my questions, I sit at my desk and look out the window. This sure is strange, communicating with men via the internet before meeting them. I quickly look back to see if I have a response back from Michigan Man. Nope—but I do have one from Devon. As I read it, I can't stop thinking about Blake. I continue the communication with Devon, and then scroll over some other matches. Again, I feel overwhelmed and start deleting matches. I respond to some of their questions, but nobody is jumping out at me like these two. I am just about to shut down my computer for the night when I see a response pop up from Blake.

His responses to my questions are amazing, almost as if he knew exactly how I'd want him to respond. The positive to this online process is that they can't roll with answers based on my facial expressions; so many people can easily manipulate a situation when in the presence of the other person. His response to the distance question is astounding, answering that if God wants to bring two people together, distance won't matter. I continue the online dating process with him, and send him the next set of questions. He responds, and we then start communicating through emails on the dating website. Although I want to give him my personal contact information, I'm still hesitant.

As I get ready for bed, I can't stop thinking about Blake. There is something that is clicking with him. He is a little older, which I actually like—it means that he's over the typical game-playing bullshit. And he has kids, which means he's probably not into having more—not that I wouldn't want more, of course, if God wants me to. He is an architect, a profession I have always admired. But what I really like is that he seems to be a dedicated man of God, a true Christian man, living as a Christian man. He's involved in missions trips, church groups, and is hungry for God's Word. He tells me he likes to listen to a daily podcast about the Bible. This is exactly the sort of man I have been praying for. *Wow—could this really be happening?* After I say my prayers, I doze off with him in my thoughts…

*********

It's a bit chilly when I wake up, so I take a little longer to pull myself out of bed. Today, I have a client meeting, physical therapy, and possibly tea with my friend Gavin. Instead of heading downstairs for my coffee right away, I jump into the shower hoping to wake myself up. Afterwards, I check my dating website email—there is one from each man. Devon wants to meet me for dinner, and it looks like he's willing to come down here to meet me—very nice. He seems like a good guy, but I'm just not that physically attracted to him in his photos, and I don't have the natural click I have with Blake.

I respond to Devon telling him I'm available tomorrow night, and then I notice I have an email from Blake. It's a long message that goes in depth about who he is and his background. I am even more interested now. It's disappointing that he is so far away—otherwise I'd be asking him to meet for coffee today! I laugh at myself and then remember to thank God; I haven't felt this way in a very long time. Every time I think about him or read a message from him, I get butterflies and want to jump up and down and go all giddy. I respond to his email and then give him my personal email address. I don't want to continue logging on to the dating site; it makes me feel weird every time, as if I'm pimping myself out. I also give Devon my personal contact information, as we'll be meeting soon anyway.

The following day I meet Devon for dinner not too far from my house. As I walk up to the front door, I see him waiting for me. He's a bit shorter than I expected and has facial hair, which his pictures had not shown, but he's still handsome.

"Hi, Anne!" He smiles and gives me a hug.

"Hi! So good to meet you in person."

We walk inside and get seated right away. The night goes really well as we share with each other more about our lives. He seems to have a great relationship with his ex-wife, a steady job, and lovely kids, but for some reason, I keep thinking about Blake. The night ends well with a kiss on the cheek and the possibility of a second date.

As I get in my car, I look at my phone to see there is a message from Blake. He is thinking about me and is hoping to chat this week. I smile with butterflies in my stomach and start to feel bad about being out with another guy. At least now I know that I should probably stop seeing Devon to see where this is going with Blake. It's just not fair to Devon; he's a good guy and deserves a woman that is into him as much as I'm into Blake.

I quickly text back: *Sorry I missed your call. You're probably in bed now. I'll call you in the morning.*

As I head home, I pray. *Thank You, God, for blessing me with new opportunities in my life. Please guide me to stay focused on You.*

# second chances

I open my eyes to see the sun's rays coming through the blinds. Wondering if Blake texted back, I reach across to pick up my phone and see a message from him.

*Good morning, Anne. Sorry—I went to bed early last night. Can I call you at three your time?*

It feels so good to wake up to a text from him. I smile as I text him back. *No worries. Yes, three is good. TTYL.*

The day feels different as I move about doing my daily routine. I'm more chipper and content, almost as if nothing can bring me down. I can't stop thinking about Blake and wondering if his voice is going to match his personality. *What if he sounds weird with a screeching voice?* Three o'clock can't come soon enough.

As three rolls around, my phone rings. "Hello?"

"Hi, Anne. This is Blake." His voice is deep and seductive. This could be the whole package.

"Hi, Blake. It is so good to hear your voice."

"It's nice to hear yours, Anne. Do I sound like what you had thought?"

"I guess so; maybe better. How about mine?"

"It sounds lovely, Anne. How's your day been?"

"Busy, but good. I had physical therapy earlier so it makes for a hectic day." I smile thinking about his voice. Thank God it's normal. "How's your day been? It's six o'clock there now, right?"

"Yes, it's six. I'm heading home from work. My office is downtown Chicago, so my drive home is about thirty minutes, depending on traffic. How was physical therapy? Does it hurt?"

"That's not too bad of a drive. No, I actually love it. I see physical therapy as a chance to get personal training, but from experts. I'm on a mission to get in better shape than before I broke my back."

"I'm impressed that you're able to be so positive about something so challenging."

"Thanks. God gave me a second chance at life and now a new body, so I'm not going to let that pass me by!"

"That's incredible. So any plans this evening?"

"No, I'll probably stay home and work tonight—nothing exciting. You?"

"I'm meeting my kids for drinks," he laughs. "That makes me sound old." He pauses. "Anne, how do you feel about that? I am much older than you."

"Gosh, it doesn't bother me at all. My ex-husband was fourteen years old than me, and I've always dated older men. Well, my ex-boyfriend was a couple years younger than me, but that obviously didn't work out. How do you feel about it?" I realize as I say that that it was a stupid question. Of course he doesn't mind dating a younger woman—*ha!* Every man would love to have some hot young woman on his arm.

"I've always dated younger women as well. My ex-wife was quite a bit younger than you. I hope I didn't get too personal asking that question; I just want to be sure you're ok with it."

"Don't worry. It's something that should be discussed. I'm glad you brought it up, Blake."

"I'm pulling into my apartment now and have a lot to do before meeting up with my kids. Can I call you tomorrow?"

"Yes, of course. Have a fun night."

"You, too. Don't work too hard."

We end the call, and I look out the window. I've been sitting here at my desk waiting to hear from him. I am so relieved that our first conversation went so well. He really seems like a great guy.

The next couple weeks leading up to Thanksgiving go by with a blur. The excitement of seeing my sister and spending time with her now that I'm healing is beyond my wildest dreams, especially after what happened five months ago. Business picks up as I learn to juggle my time between my current clients, potential clients, and of course physical therapy. Blake and I continue to get to know each other by talking every day. Although we live in two different time zones, we make it work. I text him before I go to bed so that he wakes up with a text from me, and he texts me when he wakes up. I look forward to waking up to his text messages every morning.

As I learn more about Blake, I find out that he has been married twice. His first marriage lasted fifteen years, during which they had adopted their two kids, both grown and living on their own now. He was married to his second wife for ten years and says that they both had their faults. I didn't dig deeper into the faults because I figured he would share when he felt ready. Blake travels a lot for his business but wants eventually to retire and work in the mission field full time. He hasn't been a Christian long but desires to work closely with God when the time is right. Each time we talk, I feel more closely connected to him, which is weird, because we have never met in person. As much as I want to go out to Michigan to meet him, I feel that he should be the first one to take the step. He talks about coming out to meet me but still hasn't bought his ticket yet. I don't want get my hopes up too high. I have a bad habit of jumping into things too quickly; I don't want to make the same mistake this time around.

My thoughts are interrupted when my phone rings. "Hello?"

"Hi, Anne. What are your plans for Thanksgiving?" Tami asks on the other end of the line.

"Remember, my sister Olivia is coming out here with her husband Luke. What are you doing? Is your brother having it at his new house this year?"

"Oh yeah, I forgot. No, they're going to Big Bear for the week." She sounds disappointed.

"That's a bummer. It's your first year back here. Why don't you spend Thanksgiving with us? We would love to have you over. Tell your parents they're invited, too!" The thought of having a house full of friends and family on Thanksgiving sounds wonderful; this could be my best year yet.

"Really? You don't mind if we all come? I'm sure my parents would love that." She pauses. "What can we bring? Can I bring my famous mashed potatoes?"

"Yeah, that would be great, and maybe a vegetable."

"Ok, this will be fun! Oh hey, have you heard from Blake? Is he going to come out here and meet you yet?"

"Yes, we talk every day. It is crazy how much we are talking. I really like him, T."

"Soooo, is he going to finally get his ass out here?" She laughs to lighten it up, but I can sense her seriousness.

"He told me that he might come out the weekend after Thanksgiving, but it's odd that he hasn't bought a ticket yet."

"That's weird—Thanksgiving is next week!"

"Yeah, I don't want to pressure him, but maybe I'll bring it up again tonight when we talk."

"You should! You can't just wait around for him; if he's not trying to come out here to meet you, then he's probably not into you."

"True, but he has been traveling for business and we talk every day. I think he's just busy."

"Okay, good. I just want you to be happy."

"Thanks, T; I really appreciate your honesty and your friendship."

"When does your sister arrive?"

"Tomorrow. Crazy how time has flown. I am really looking forward to seeing her. Last time I was still living out of my hospital bed."

"She'll be so proud of how far you've come. Let me know if you guys end up going out. I'd love to hang out before the chaos of Thanksgiving."

"Okay. Not sure if we will, but I'll let you know if we do."

Just as I end the conversation, Blake calls. I am thrilled when he tells me he's booking a ticket to come out to visit me the weekend of Thanksgiving. Cruz will be at his dad's and my sister flies home the morning after Thanksgiving. He will be here for three days, which I think will be a perfect amount of time to see whether or not there is a connection. He will be staying at a hotel down the street from me; thankfully, he didn't expect to stay at my house. Although I am excited that he finally bought a ticket, I'm also a little scared that it all rides on this one meeting—if we don't click, then all this time will have been for nothing.

The day flies by and before I know it, Cruz and I are on our way to the airport.

"Mom, do you think Uncle Luke brought his PlayStation?"

I laugh. "I'm not sure." My brother-in-law has always been a kid at heart, playing video games on his own time, which makes for a perfect visit, because he plays with Cruz while Olivia and I get to do girl things.

We pull into the airport to see them standing along the side of the curb, Olivia wearing a purple sweater and Luke wearing his traditional green Oregon sweatshirt. The two of them always look so cute together. Before I come to a full stop, Cruz opens the car door and runs over to Luke, hugging him.

I walk to the back of the car to help them load their bags and see Olivia. She smiles. "Anne, you look so good!" We hug and stand there looking at each other. Tears start to fill my eyes.

"You have no idea how good it is to see you. I've missed you."

"Me, too. Sorry we couldn't come down sooner."

Luke gives me a hug. "You look really good! Can't believe you just broke your back six months ago."

"Thanks. I feel great!"

Olivia tells me about all the family gossip on the way home and how it's good to be spending time away from all of it for a change. It's late when we get home, but it doesn't stop us from catching up. Luke and Cruz play video games while Olivia and I chat over a bottle of wine in front of the fireplace. I've only told Tami about Blake, mostly because we met on a dating website, and because I haven't met him in person yet and don't want to get anyone's hopes up. Olivia and I talk about my expectations, and if the first date goes well, what we should do the rest of the time he's here.

After finishing a second bottle of wine, we decide to call it a night and head up to bed. Just as I start to fall asleep, I text Blake.

*Good morning! Had a nice night with my sis—great catching up with her. Have a blessed day!*

I smile when I read Blake's text the following day. *Good morning, Anne. I can't wait to see you. Have a blessed day.*

There's also a text from Jack, my old neighbor, asking me if I want to come over for coffee. Ever since my surgery, he has been a big part of my spiritual journey, inspiring and lifting my spirits with positive advice and encouraging words. I consider him my spiritual mentor.

*Thanks for the invite, but my sister and brother-in-law are here visiting. I'm about to make breakfast. Do you want to come over?*

He replies, *Sure. What can I bring?*

*Just yourself.*

As I walk downstairs, I see Cruz playing video games in his room.

"Hey, bud. I'm about to make breakfast. Do you want pancakes?"

"Yes—and sausage!" He looks up at me briefly with a big smile. "Please."

I walk into the kitchen and start preparing the pancake batter just as I get a knock on the door. Wiping my hands with a towel, I head to the door to see that it's Jack. Grinning from ear to ear, I give him a big hug.

"Good to see you, too," he says, holding me tightly.

"My sister and her husband are still asleep. Do you want some coffee?"

"Sure, love. How can I help?"

He follows me into the kitchen, where we make coffee and chat about life. We talk about Blake's upcoming visit, and he gives me advice on how to stay positive even if it's not what I expect.

"I have a really good feeling about him. He could be the one."

Jack smiles. "Don't get ahead of yourself, Anne. Stay in the present. You're having a good time getting to know him; don't let it be any more than what it is."

"True." Jack always seems to know how to get me back to reality.

Olivia walks into the kitchen with Luke not too far behind. "Good morning!"

"Do you remember Jack?" I ask as they acknowledge each other.

"I remember Jack," Olivia says, giving him a hug. "You came over to see Anne after her surgery."

"Yes, that was me."

"This is my husband, Luke."

"Nice meeting you." They shake hands.

"You guys up for some breakfast? Anne and I are going to make a breakfast of champions."

"Starving!" Olivia and Luke say in unison.

\*\*\*\*\*\*\*\*\*\*

Over the next several days, we lie low and hang out at the house. Olivia isn't feeling well, which doesn't seem to bother Luke because he is content staying home and playing video games with Cruz. The days run together, as I am awaiting Blake's arrival. I almost feel bad because I should be spending quality time with my family, but with Olivia sick, there isn't much we can do but lie around the house and drink tea. This isn't what I had expected their visit to be like, but it's certainly nice having them here.

The day before Thanksgiving, Olivia and I sit down to go over our menu. Tami wants to come over and help early in the morning, but I want to make sure we have all the bases covered. I will make the turkey while Olivia makes the stuffing, and Tami will bring the mashed potatoes. She is also bringing her parents, which will make it a dinner party of seven, including Cruz. Usually I split the day with his dad, but this year I get him the entire day because Jeff will be out of town.

"I have a really good idea for the table. You know how it's typical of people going around the table telling everyone what they are thankful for?" Olivia asks me.

"Yeah?"

"I think we should give everyone a river rock, and then I will read them the book of Joshua, where after he crossed the river Jordan, God asked the high priests to build a memorial of rocks representing what God had done for them. We will then ask everyone to write on their rock one word that represents what God has done for them this past year."

"That sounds awesome. We can use the rocks I have out on the patio." I point outside.

"Perfect."

"Anything else we should do?"

"Nope. I think we have it all covered. I'm still not feeling well. I hope you don't mind, but I'm going to head upstairs to take a nap."

"No problem. I have some grocery shopping that I need to do. Go rest up."

**********

Thanksgiving Day flies by. All the food turns out well, and the plan for giving thanks to God with the river rocks is a success. We stay up late taking about past holidays and chaotic family gatherings; the house is full of laughter and love. I can't imagine it being any better. As I go to bed, I thank God for the opportunity to be here with my family and friends. It's been a long six months, but this is all worth it.

The following morning, we drop Cruz off at his dad's on the way to the airport. Cruz is sad to be leaving, but his sadness is blunted by the fact that Olivia and Luke are also going home. On the way, Olivia and I try to plan their next visit—we hope for the spring.

After I drop them off and the car is quiet, I start to cry. The emotions have built up and I am overcome with gratitude. My sister has done so much for me this last year; I am so blessed to have her in my life, so blessed to still be around. *Thank You, God, for saving me from that jump; thank You for giving me this second chance at life. This could have been a much different holiday for my family. Thank You.*

I spend the rest of the day cleaning up around the house. Blake is coming tomorrow and I want everything to be nice just in case I invite him inside. He will be staying at the hotel down the road from my house—but who knows? We might want to stay in one night and make dinner. I want to be prepared for anything.

**********

Through all the excitement and anxiety, I am unable to sleep much. I wake up early and go for a long walk, thinking about all the things Blake and I could do this weekend. Luckily it's going to be a beautiful weekend, staying around the high seventies, which is not normal this time of year— but I will take it. Blake will be flying in this evening, so the plan is to meet for dinner and drinks.

*188*

I decide to spend the rest of my day working and staying focused on other things, keeping my mind off him. The day flies by, and before I know it, it's time to get ready for the date. I jump in the shower, making sure to take time grooming; I am not going to get physical with him, but I do want to look and feel good. Just as I get out of the shower, my phone rings. It's him.

I dry off my hands and grab the phone. "Hi, Blake! Welcome to Cali!"

"Thank you. I just landed." There's a pause. "You still want to meet? You haven't changed your mind yet?" I can sense uneasiness on his end.

"Of course I want to meet you!" I joke, "Nooo, I changed my mind. Go home."

He laughs. "Ok. Cool. I'm heading to pick up my rental car now. Do you want to meet at the hotel lobby in an hour?"

"Sure. See you there."

I look in the mirror and smile. I am dripping wet, but it doesn't bother me—I am so excited to see him in person.

Before my sister left, she had helped me pick out an outfit, deciding on designer jeans and a low-cut black sweater. She told me that since it's our first date, I shouldn't show too much off. "Don't give it all away on the first date; otherwise he won't have anything to look forward to on the second." I laugh as I put my sweater over my head.

Just as I head out the door, I take a selfie and text it to Tami. *Wish me luck!*

The drive to the hotel is faster than I had thought, so I text Blake. *I'm here. Take your time. I'll be in the bar.*

He texts back, *Ok. I'll be down in fifteen minutes.*

The room is empty when I walk in and look around. Where to sit? I decide on the bar, hoping to chat with the bartender to keep my mind off the big moment.

"I would like your house Pinot Noir." Fortunately there is a mirror on the wall, so I can see who is coming in from behind me. This will be a perfect position to see Blake when he walks in.

"Here you go, miss," the bartender says, placing the glass of wine in front of me.

I sip the wine and say a prayer. *Please give me the right words to say and help me be myself. Give us both the wisdom to make the right decisions tonight.* I have to say that because I am very attracted to him. If I get swept away in the moment and he is the type of guy to push it, then I need God's strength to say no.

An older man at the end of the bar tries to start small talk with me, but I keep looking over my shoulder at the entrance to the bar as if to show him that I am not interested. Normally I would talk it up, but I don't want to give Blake the wrong impression. Just as I look at my phone to see the time, out of the corner of my eye I see a man walk in wearing a blazer and jeans. I cannot see his face clearly, though, so I slightly turn to look when I feel a tap on my other shoulder. "Anne?"

"Oh my gosh! Blake!" I wasn't sure what I would do when I met him in person for the first time, but suddenly I feel like hugging him. We hold on to each other for a couple minutes and then he pulls me away, still holding onto my shoulders. "Is this you? I can't believe it!" He leans down to kiss my cheek. He is taller than I had imagined, standing at six-two, with broad shoulders and a supreme posture. He is dressed nicely in dark blue jeans, custom button down shirt, and black sports coat.

Sitting down next to me, he orders a glass of wine. He is more handsome than I had thought; his pictures didn't do him justice. "So . . . am I what you imagined?"

Looking at him I grab his hand and laugh. "Much better!"

"Really?" he responds tightening his grip around my hand.

"Yes. What about me?"

"Exactly what I had thought—beautiful." He pulls my hand up to his lips and kisses it.

"What next? Are you hungry?"

"Absolutely. Let's go somewhere quiet."

We head downtown to Huntington Beach and end up at a small Italian restaurant. Everything is surreal; it seems like a dream come true. I've finally met a guy who is the whole package. We share childhood stories and laugh all night; the waiter has to ask us to leave because they're closing up.

The night ends back at the hotel, where I drop him off and give him a hug. I so badly want to kiss him, but he doesn't make the move, so I settle for memories of an amazing evening.

That night I lie in my bed thinking about the night with Blake and anticipating the following day. For the first time ever, I am going to church with a guy that I am totally into. I fall asleep dreaming about the future…

**********

Blake picks me up right on time. Score. I like it when a man can be reliable—it says a lot about his character. Although my home church is around the corner, we had talked about going to Saddleback because he had done some outreach work through them a while back, so I surprise him with a tour of the church before the service starts. To top his experience, a popular Christian music group happens to play at the service.

"Anne, that was amazing!" exclaims Blake, grabbing my hand as we walk to his rental car.

"I thought you would like it!"

He walks around to open my door, as he has been doing. "Where to now?"

"Let's go to Laguna Beach—it's such a beautiful day."

The drive to the beach is scenic, with views of the hills through Lake Forest to the cliffs of Laguna. We end up at the Roof Top, a popular eatery.

"This way," I say, pulling Blake's hand in my direction. We walk up the stairs following the signs to the roof top. The stairs lead to a small dark room with a door; I push the door open to see sunlight.

"Whoa, blinding!" I laugh, covering my face.

"Look at this view," Blake whispers into my ear.

There is a Tiki bar along one side of the roof and tall bistro tables with white table cloths surrounding the bar. Every table has a view of the beach going as far north and south as I can see.

"Let's sit here." He pulls out a chair at a table along the edge of the roof.

"Thanks."

We order some mojitos and look over the menu.

"Do you like shrimp?" Blake points at a dish listed on the menu.

"Yes. Let's get that," I smile, sipping my drink.

We order and start to chat about the sermon we heard at church, and then he tells me that he doesn't have a home church because he hasn't been home enough to connect with any particular church. I feel for him because—despite any past problems—I've been blessed with a fundamentally good church and I can't imagine having to find one to connect with.

"Excuse me." The waiter is standing over the table with a tray of food. "Shrimp cocktail, chicken satay, and seafood ceviche?"

"Yes, right here." Blake makes room at the table as the waiter places the food down.

"This looks good," I say.

We eat while talking about our hopes and dreams, which are similar. He wants to travel the world and do missions work, while I want to travel the world telling my story, working for God in whatever way I can. As the conversation about our dreams starts winding down, I can sense Blake wants to say something.

"Anne . . . I need to be honest with you."

*Oh gosh, here it comes—he's married.*

"You know that I've been married twice. Well, the second marriage didn't end quite so nicely." He pauses. "I cheated on her." He looks down and away. I can see the shame on his face.

"Oh," is all I can say. Thankfully, he breaks the awkward silence.

"It was one time—a big mistake. We were both spending too much time apart and I got weak." He puts his hand on top of mine on the table. "I ended up telling my ex and she couldn't forgive me. She couldn't get past it."

"Gosh, I'm sorry. Have you forgiven yourself?"

"Yes. It was hard, and it took a long time, but I've gotten over it—but I wanted to tell you because I think it's important that you know."

"Thank you. I appreciate your honesty."

Just as it is getting awkward, the waiter comes by to clear the dishes as we order another round of drinks. We change the subject and talk about our kids, a much brighter topic.

"Let's watch the sunset here and then head back to Huntington," Blake suggests, pulling his chair closer to mine.

"Sounds good."

"I could live here," Blake says, turning to me. "I'd just have to figure out what I'd do for a job. I guess I could do some contract work."

"Really? You would move here?" I had never asked directly about the possibility of his moving because he had stated in his online profile that he would move if he met the right one.

"Yes, I'd love to live here—if this is where God wants me."

He smiles and looks at me. "May I kiss you?"

Without responding, I move in for the kiss. He pulls me into him, grabbing the back of my neck; his lips so delicately touch mine. I feel a spark and butterflies in my stomach. We've waited too long for this.

He pulls away. "I've wanted to do that since I saw you in the hotel bar."

"You should have. That was really nice." I lean in to kiss him again.

We stay to watch the sun go down and then head back to my house, where he drops me off to get dressed for dinner. We have reservations at an Indian restaurant in Long Beach, and since we spent more time than expected in Laguna, we will have to rush getting ready for dinner.

Twenty minutes later Blake is back at my door wearing another sports jacket, looking quite handsome as usual.

The drive to dinner is quiet, so I break the silence. "What time is your flight tomorrow?"

"I need to look, but I think it's at two o'clock."

"Okay. It gives us a little time to do something."

I want to say that I'll miss him, but I wonder if it's too soon for me to express my emotions; some guys get skittish about it. Although we've hit it off and it seems like he's into me as much as I am into him, I don't want to risk it.

Dinner is fabulous; he had researched the restaurant ahead of time, knowing that I like Indian food. After dinner we end up back at my house. I've decided to let him in since it is our last night.

While Blake is in the bathroom, I light candles around the fireplace and in the kitchen, which is part of the family room. When he returns, I hand him a glass of wine.

"You were drinking Cabernet, so I thought that you would like this *BV Georges de Latour.*"

He takes it from my hand and sets it down on the counter. "I'd rather have some of this Latour," he says, wrapping his arms around me, pulling me into him. I look up at him and smile just as he leans down to kiss me. This time we don't have an audience, so I kiss him back deeply.

After a while, we slow things down and walk into the family room. I sit on the couch wondering what I should do next—turn on the TV or music. I decide on the music, playing some Christian R&B.

Blake sits down next to me putting his hand on my leg. "Anne, you can say no, but can I see your back?"

"Sure." Slowly I lift the back of my shirt up so he can see the scar. "It must have

"Yep—nine hours."

"I am so sorry you had to go through that," I can hear the sincerity in his voice, almost as if he is sad.

"No, don't be sorry. I thank God for it. I am a better person now."

I turn to look at him, thinking he is done looking at my back, but he turns me back around and starts to kiss the back of my neck. *Oh gosh, this isn't good—my sweet spot. Lord, please help me to stay strong.* He continues to kiss my neck, slowly pulling my shirt up over my head. He unbuckles my bra and kisses down my back as he gently pushes me towards the cushions of the couch.

"Do you mind if I kiss your back?" he asks, kissing my shoulders.

"No . . . Go ahead." I barely get the words out. This is so romantic. He's kissing my scar in the moonlit candlelight—and I really like him.

He continues to kiss down my back, seductively massaging my shoulders and then slowly turns me over, coming back up to kiss my lips. I kiss him back passionately, as I am dying to have his lips on mine again. I pull off his shirt and start to nibble on his ear and then move down to his neck. His body is soft and tastes sweeter with every kiss. All of a sudden Blake pulls back.

"Anne, I really want you right now—all of you—but I don't want to cross any boundaries."

I sit up and look at him. Who is this guy? It's like he came straight from heaven.

"I'm glad you said something, because I am saving myself. I'm not sure what it'll look like, but I feel that since my accident, God wants me to be married before I have sex."

Blake sits back as he listens to me. "Okay."

I continue, "I haven't had sex for six months. I am waiting for God to bring me the right man. He has promised me."

"Well, what does God say about me?"

"I don't know yet—but I know I really like you." I lean over and kiss him while grabbing my shirt.

"I'm sorry if I pushed things tonight," he says, buttoning up his shirt.

"No, don't be sorry. I'm glad we talked about it."

He leaves not too much longer after our discussion. I tell him how I used to live my life and the relationship I was in. I explain that I am looking for something solid, something long-term, but mostly something that God would be proud of.

**********

The next morning Blake shows up with flowers and Starbucks coffee. After talking for a short while about the previous night, we decide on walking to the beach. The walk down is nice, holding hands and talking about the future. He says he wants to come back soon and would love for me to fly out to Michigan to meet his kids. We talk about the countries we want to visit and the work we could do for God. After spending some time talking at the beach, we head back to say our good-byes. The walk back is quiet, as I'm sure the departure is as much on his mind as it is on mine.

We reach the house and stand inside my entryway looking at each other. Blake pulls me in close and wraps his arms around me. "I have had an amazing time, Anne. I never thought I would feel this way when meeting you. Thank you for everything."

"No, thank *you*." I hold him tighter. "You have given me hope. Thank you."

He pulls back enough to reach down for a kiss, one last kiss. It is soft and tender yet ardent. I can feel the electricity run through my body. After he leaves, I walk into the house and plop on the couch. Although I am sad to see Blake go, I feel enlightened.

**********

All this time God has been telling me to listen to Him, to focus on Him. He promised me that my dreams would come true if I would focus on Him, and yet I was stubborn. I'd like to think that God shook me so hard in the ocean that I broke my back. If I hadn't broken my back, I would not have met Blake. I'd still be doing circles around Dave, wondering why God hadn't brought a real man into my life. Spending these past few days with Blake makes me realize what I have been missing—what I deserve as a woman. He makes me feel important and wanted; he also makes me feel appreciated, but most importantly, he respects me.

I kept asking God why he allowed everything to happen and yet, I realize that all this time, all He wanted from me was to put Him first. From the moment I heard my dad had committed suicide to the moment I broke my back, I called on others. Literally I picked up the phone and called people, when all I had to do was pray. God was there all along, waiting on me.

Looking back I feel bad… how much it must have broken His heart when I failed to call on Him first. He is all so knowing and all so powerful, if anyone can comfort us or create a miracle… it is God. It doesn't matter how small the problem, He is always here for us.

God gave me a second chance at life when I came out of that ocean. Then He gave me a second chance at walking when I came out of surgery. Now He has given me a second chance at love. It is up to me to keep my promise to God, serving Him with all of my heart. As it says in John 5:14, "After this, Jesus found him in the temple area and said to him, 'Look you are well; do not sin any more, so that nothing worse may happen to you.'" Miraculously God has given me full use of my body, not to serve my sensual appetite for sin, but to serve Him in purity and holiness, with peace and joy.

# *Afterthoughts*

During the writing of this book, I did a lot of soul searching. Over a six-month period, I was blessed with the ability to make several life-changing decisions. I followed God's calling to another country, where I miraculously survived a terrible jump. Instead of being angry at God or the church, I continued to follow Him without prejudice. If God has the power to save me from paralysis, how could I not continue to trust Him?

Throughout my recovery and even still today, everyone asks me how I did it. They would say, "How did you stay so positive?" or "How did you recover so quickly?" My answer has always been: grace. "God covered me in grace." To be perfectly honest with you, in the beginning I didn't know why I would answer it that way. I would find myself just blurting it out. It's strange, because up until that point I never really knew what grace was, nor had I used it in a sentence before. It wasn't until I read Max Lucado's book *Grace* that I realized I had literally been drenched in the grace of God. I still can't clearly describe grace, but I can tell you that it just happens. It is a divine intervention during a rough time; it is a calmness you get when you pray to God; or it could be the smile you see on a child's face. I was blessed by the grace of God.

With that being said, if I could go back in time to that cliff in Indonesia, I would do it all over again the exact same way. I was living my life in a selfish and reckless way. As much as I thought I was putting God first, I wasn't. He had plans for me, and yet I wasn't following His direction. He had to re-direct me.

Would you consider that a wake-up call? I have.

God has been telling me for years now to slow down and focus on Him, especially when it comes to relationships. He has told me if I just stop and focus on Him, He will bring the perfect man into my life. Instead, I let greed and sexual desire rule my decision process.

It's tough being a divorced single mom. Dating is much different for mid-thirties women these days; so much is expected of us. How are we supposed to stay pure until marriage when we've already experienced sex? That intimate feeling we get when we are with a man, that feeling of closeness and belonging—God created woman to want that and need it, but under *His* terms. As it says in Hebrews 13:4, "Let marriage be held in honor among all, and let the marriage bed be undefiled, for God will judge the sexually immoral and adulterous." Could this be why fifty percent of marriages fail in the United States? And the failure rate is even higher for those who marry a second or third time.

One might say, "But it is impossible these days to stay pure before marriage." One might even stress the societal impact sex has on today's relationships. Heck, you can't even turn the TV or radio on, let alone drive down the street, without seeing something related to sex. Could purity be impossible?

Let's visit the Bible verse Matthew 19:26, when Jesus said, "With people this is impossible, but with God all things are possible." Since I have personally experienced the miracles of God's divine power, I truly believe that it is possible to stay pure before marriage. It won't be easy—but if you rely on God moment by moment by keeping Him close to your heart, if you talk with Him often as with a friend, and if you commit yourself to avoiding occasions that could lead to trouble, God will surely give us the grace to stay true to His commands. And when we live only to please God, He will bless us in abundance.

*Put God first by praying this prayer every day:*
I lift my eyes to You Lord.
Let all my distractions slip away.
May my belief in You, my hope in You, my trust in You, be my focal point.
When my mind starts to drift away from You, bring me back to You.
Help train my mind to seek Your guidance, in each moment of every day.
May the path I walk be obedient steps in accordance with Your will for my life.
Amen.

# Let's Connect

AnneLatour.com

## FACEBOOK
facebook.com/BaliGirlBook

## TWITTER
@AnneLatourHB

## INSTAGRAM
AnneLatourHB

## PINTEREST
pinterest.com/annelatourhb/

## EMAIL
anne@AnneLatour.com